D1105105

10-23-75

SYSTEM AND FUNCTION
Toward a Theory of Society

STUDIES IN ANTHROPOLOGY

Under the Consulting Editorship of E. A. Hammel,
UNIVERSITY OF CALIFORNIA, BERKELEY

SYSTEM
AND FUNCTION
Toward a Theory of Society

PIOTR SZTOMPKA

Krakow University
Krakow, Poland

ACADEMIC PRESS   New York San Francisco London

A Subsidiary of Harcourt Brace Jovanovich, Publishers

ACADEMIC PRESS, INC.
111 Fifth Avenue, New York, New York 10003

United Kingdom Edition published by
ACADEMIC PRESS, INC. (LONDON) LTD.
24/28 Oval Road, London NW1

Library of Congress Cataloging in Publication Data

Sztompka, Piotr.
    System and function.

    (Studies in anthropology series)
    Bibliography: p.
    1.   Functional analysis (Social sciences)
2.   System theory.   3.   Social systems.   I.   Title.
HM24.S954   301'.01   74-1644
ISBN 0–12–681850–9

1882723

To
  my wife, my mother, and my Polish friends—
  whom I missed while working on this book.

CONTENTS

PREFACE

This book springs from two convictions. First, I believe that the best single index of the maturity of a scientific discipline, considered as the total of scientific results, is the state of general theory. And second, I believe that the best single index of the maturity of a scientific discipline, considered as the ongoing research enterprise, is the professed attitude among the scientific community toward general theory. In light of these criteria it seems that sociology in the 1970s is at last coming of age.

Even if we are still far from having an adequate theory of social phenomena, the corpus of generalized propositions well rooted in empirical research has grown enormously. And despite the much publicized attempts to steer the course of sociology out of the domain of science back into speculative, subjectivist obscurantism, these tendencies are obviously contrary to the growing consensus in sociology that concerns the theoretical goals of our discipline.

The spurious dilemma of theory versus research, which has pervaded the history of sociology for more than a century, finds its solution in the notion of empirical theory conceived as a system of propositions derived from empirical research and tested in empirical research. We have hopefully outgrown both theorizing without data and data collection without theory. The time has come to face the old task in a new way. We must again attempt to build a general theory of society, but this time, an empirical theory.

The general empirical theory of society may be conceived as the adequate answer to the following questions:

1. Why do societies keep together and persist? (This is sometimes referred to as the Hobbesian problem.)
2. Why do societies fall apart and change? (This is sometimes referred to as the Marxian problem.)

Any attempt to answer these questions must begin with the clarification of two interlinked issues. The first issue is *formal;* it concerns the structure that an adequate scientific answer must have. Briefly, it demands the syntactic definition of a *theory.* The second issue is *substantive;* it concerns the language in which an adequate scientific answer must be phrased. That is, it demands the semantic specification of a *conceptual model.*

This book deals with both preliminary issues. It does not provide a theory of society, yet it does suggest a logical form in which such a theory should be cast, as well as the conceptual raw material with which the theoretical form should be filled.

The direction of theory construction that will be outlined here is the continuation of two traditions of modern sociological thinking. With respect to the form of a theory, I attempt to explicate, elaborate, and develop the *explanatory notion of a theory* that is perhaps best defended by George C. Homans. And with respect to the language of a theory, I attempt to reconstruct, elaborate, and develop the *systemic–functional conceptual models* that are perhaps most explicitly outlined within the functionalist school in sociology and social anthropology, from Bronislaw Malinowski to Talcott Parsons.

I believe that the notion of a theory as a system of explanations makes up the most realistic minimum standard of scientific endeavor at the present stage of social science; the standard which it is at least conceivable to achieve and which is also fully congruent with, or even conducive to, the ultimate ideal of a formalized, deductive system of propositions. And I believe that the conceptualization of social reality in systemic–functional terms makes up the most fruitful approach to both questions that are central for the theory of society: the question of order and persistence, as well as that of conflict and change.

In light of the sociological disputes of the past two decades it should be immediately apparent that I am attempting to reconcile the seemingly irreconcilable and to bridge the seemingly unbridge-able. It may be pointed out that Homans's comments on the form of sociological theory were self-consciously directed against the types of results typically achieved within the functionalist school. The notion of a theory as a system of explanations was conceived as contradictory to the notion of theory as a set of analytic categories. I object to this presumption. Accepting Homans's idea of theory, I try to show that the specification of a conceptual model is a necessary precondition of a theory understood precisely in his sense. Thus, whereas it is certainly improper to consider a set of analytic categories as the ulti-mate goal of sociological research, the conceptual model has a decisive instrumental significance in the process of theory construction.

However, it may also be pointed out that the functionalist concep-tual model is usually charged with a static and ahistoric bias and as a result seems basically unable to handle the Marxian question of conflict and change, even if it can give some illumination to the Hobbesian problem of order and persistence. I reject both claims. In this volume I argue that these particular theoretical biases were certainly characteristic of some implementations of the systemic–func-tional model, but they are neither necessary nor principal defects of the model as such. I attempt to reconstruct and generalize the conceptual model characteristic to the functionalist orientation and to disentangle it from specific implementations, in order to render it immune to any of these criticisms and to transform it into a neutral, analytically powerful instrument for handling order and conflict, per-sistence and change.

Moreover I will attempt to establish that it was Karl Marx himself who applied most successfully the generalized systemic–functional model to the dynamic and historic study of human society. This asser-tion admittedly may provoke those antifunctionalists who try to sell their own subjectivistic, idealistic, and muddled views under the mis-leading cover of "new Marxism."

Before setting off on my course there are some intellectual debts to be acknowledged. This book is primarily a reconstruction, and at most a critical and postulative reconstruction. Obviously, one could not reconstruct if there were nothing from which to reconstruct. Hence, my first and foremost debt is to the creators of that particular methodological and theoretical tradition from which I draw and which I try to further. This debt is duly recognized in the references and in the bibliography.

My more personal gratitude is due to all those who challenged my ideas and thereby contributed much to their clarification. Among many others I would like to mention specifically Professor Klemens Szaniawski and Professor Jerzy Wiatr, who read some parts of the manuscript and made invaluable comments. The students in my course in sociological theory at the Jagiellonian University in Krakow, Poland, became the experimental subjects on whom I tested the perception of my more controversial points: therefore, they also contributed to the present result.

The preparation of the English version of the book was made possible by the stimulating environment of the University of California, Berkeley, where I visited as a Fulbright Research Fellow during the academic year 1972–1973. Here, I especially appreciated the friendly help given to me by Professor Neil J. Smelser. Involved disputes with a group of graduate students, and particularly Erik Wright, proved very useful, too.

Finally, as I firmly believe the contributions of all the persons mentioned above were purely positive, the full responsibility for the remaining deficiencies of the argument rests solely with myself.

QUOTATION CREDITS

The author gratefully acknowledges permission to reprint excerpts from the following works.

Ackerman, C. and T. Parsons, The concept of social system as a theoretical device. In *Concepts, Theory and Explanation in the Behavioral Sciences*, pp. 24–42, edited by G. J. DeRenzo. New York: Random House, 1966. © 1966 by Random House, Inc.

Beattie, J. H. M., *Other Cultures: Aims, Methods and Achievements in Social Anthropology*. New York: Free Press, 1964. © 1964 by Free Press.

Buckley, W., *Sociology and Modern Systems Theory*. Englewood Cliffs, New Jersey: Prentice-Hall, 1967. © 1967 by Prentice-Hall, Inc.

Dahrendorf, R., *Essays in the Theory of Society*. Stanford, California: Stanford University Press, 1968.

Emmet, D., *Function, Purpose and Powers*. London: Routledge & Kegan Paul Ltd., 1958.

Geertz, C., Ritual and social change: A Javenese Example. Reproduced by permission of the American Anthropological Association from the *American Anthropologist* 59: 32–54, 1957.

Gouldner, A. W., Reciprocity and autonomy in functional theory. In *Symposium on Sociological Theory*, pp. 241–270, edited by L. Gross. New York: Harper & Row, Publishers, Inc.

Homans, G. C., *The Nature of Social Science*. New York: Harcourt Brace Jovanovich, Inc., 1967.

Homans, G. C., *Sentiments and Activities: Essays in Social Science*. New York: Free Press, 1962. © 1962 by Free Press. London: Routledge & Kegan Paul, Ltd., 1962.

Levy, M. J. Jr., *The Structure of Society*. Princeton, New Jersey: Princeton University Press. Copyright 1952 by Princeton University Press. Selections from pp. 40, 62, 65, 87, 88, 89, 122, 149, 174, 175. Reprinted by permission of Princeton University Press.

Malinowski, B., *A Scientific Theory of Culture and Other Essays*. London and New York: Oxford University Press, 1969. Copyright 1944 by University of North Carolina Press.

Meehan, E. J., *Explanation in Social Science: A System Paradigm*. Homewood, Illinois: Dorsey Press, 1968.

Merton, R. K., *On Theoretical Sociology*. New York: Free Press, 1967. © 1967 by Free Press.

Parsons, T., *The Social System*. New York: Free Press, 1951. © 1951 by Free Press.

Radcliffe-Brown, A. R., *Structure and Function in Primitive Society*. New York: Free Press, 1952. © 1952 by Free Press. London: Routledge & Kegan Paul, Ltd., 1952.

"The accomplishments of functional analysis
are sufficient to suggest that its large promise
will progressively be fulfilled, just as its
current deficiencies testify to the need for
periodically overhauling the past the better
to build for the future [Robert K. Merton, 1949: 19]."

THEORY AND MODEL IN SOCIOLOGY
Formal Framework for Theory Construction

PART I

THEORY AND MODEL IN SOCIOLOGY
Formal Construction
in a Theory Construction

Chapter 1

THEORETICAL IDEAL
IN MODERN SOCIOLOGY

In 1952 in his paper, "The Present Status of Social Theory," Theodore Abel wrote: ". . . its ascribed status must be rated as low in view of the prevailing tendency to regard discussion of social facts in general categories as an improper form of scientific reporting [p. 159]." Almost two decades later, in a paper entitled "The Present State of Theory in Sociology," R. A. Robson (1968) remarked: "Pronouncements about theory in sociology are at present almost unanimous; we are all for it [p. 368]." These statements mark two epochs in the history of postwar sociology. It seems that sociologists have reached a consensus on the basic theoretical goals of the discipline.

This consensus is based on the critical reassessment of our present achievements. What do we have, and what do we lack in sociology? Both tendencies that dominated the discipline in the postwar period, narrow empiricism and formal conceptualism, have had considerable influence. The main contribution of the empirical tendency is an enormous amount of data on social organization and human behavior. According to Sorokin (1966): "The main achievements of the recent period consist largely in excavating and analyzing an enormous mass of relevant and irrelevant empirical facts. . . [p. 648]." We are obviously rich in facts, perhaps we have too many facts; their number, specificity, and heterogeneity seem to inhibit any wider reflection. This is true of social anthropology, whose practitioners ". . . found themselves so intimidated by the sheer weight of ethnographic detail that they retreated in dismay from an essential task of theory formation, namely, abstraction. Thus, ironically, anthropology's empirical riches have tended often to act as a deterrent rather than a stimulus to theory formation [Manners and Kaplan 1968: 4]." And this is also true in sociology, which, Sorokin (1966) remarked, "has excavated so many facts that it often does not know what to do with them [p. 649]."

But our empirical heritage consists not only of singular, isolated facts. We have also many propositions summarizing empirical observations referring to the closed class of observed cases. Zetterberg (1954:47) has such generalizations in mind when he claims that despite all opinions to the contrary, sociology has set forth a large number of general propositions, and Berelson and Steiner (1964) included no less than 1045 generalizations of this type in their famous inventory.

Finally, we have also a restricted number of lawlike hypotheses, derived from empirical data and sufficiently confirmed by empirical data, but unlimited in scope; i.e., referring to the open class of cases, past, present, and future. This is acknowledged by Zetterberg (1954) ". . . apart from facts, are there in the body of sociological knowledge any laws [or lawlike propositions] that can be called confirmed or trustworthy? The answer is undoubtedly yes [p. 47]." The only problem with sociological laws is that they are usually isolated, rather than integrated into wider propositional structures.

The contribution of the formal tendency is equally great. It consists of a vast body of concepts, classifications, typologies, definitions, and the like. In Fallding's (1968) view, "Actually, the theoretical accomplishments of sociology so far have been preponderantly at this level. There is a considerable wealth yet to be counted in concept formation in the discipline [p. 25]." But this wealth is an asset, as well as a liability. As Ossowski (1962) once observed:

> A sociologist very often behaves as if the discipline was born with him; he constructs his own conceptual apparatus, poses once again the old issues, makes discoveries that have been already made, or that even entered into the corpus of common-sense knowledge, and gives them the flavor of novelty by new terminological phrasing. This conceptual and terminological anarchy sets sociology apart from the natural sciences [p. 164].

If this diagnosis is correct, sociology is currently in the phase which, in Bunge's (1967) terms, may be called "pretheoretical" and "pre-empirical [p. 380]." Then, what is lacking in sociology, and, consequently, what does it require to become a fully theoretical and fully empirical scientific discipline? Bunge (1967: 380) claims that the basic characteristic of a developed, mature science is the focus on the theoretical systematization of knowledge as opposed to raw experience. Precisely what contemporary sociology lacks and what it requires most is the *theoretical systematization* of isolated facts, generalizations, and hypotheses.

Perhaps the most consistent among the authors who perceive the current cognitive status and future perspectives of sociology in these terms is Homans. In *The Nature of Social Science*, Homans (1967) argued the case with characteristic clarity:

> It is not in its findings which are now numerous and well attested, that social science gets into trouble, but in its explanations. The trouble takes somewhat different forms in different fields, but explanation, theory, is always its seat [p. 28].

> . . . Our trouble has not been with making discoveries but with organizing them theoretically—showing how they follow under a variety of given conditions from a few general principles. That is what I have meant by saying that the problem of social science is not discovery but explanation. Only if we recognize the nature of our problem can we begin to cope with it [p. 105].

In short, we have enough facts and enough concepts, but we must still learn to speak about the world of our facts in the language of our concepts. We must give meaningful organization to the scattered elements of our sociological knowledge. The need for theoretical systematization and adequate theory construction seems to be recognized ever more clearly at the present time.

Chapter 2

THE NOTION OF
A THEORY

Vague ideals usually have no motivating power. In order to influence actual research endeavors, a theoretical ideal must be specified. In sociological usage, the notion of a theory is extremely ambiguous. Cohen (1968) remarked wryly that in sociology "the term theory is like a check in blanco. Its value depends on the user and his use of it [p. 8]." Elsewhere (Sztompka 1972) I distinguished 22 distinct meanings that the term "theory" acquires in sociological literature, and probably the list is far from complete. For present purposes I shall put aside the critical discussion of actual uses and abuses, focusing instead on the explication of the particular, selected meaning that seems most fruitful as a standard of sociological inquiry.

Such explication may be carried out in two ways: first, in a direct way, by defining the structural features (i.e., specific properties of elementary propositions and/or specific properties of their organization) that distinguish a theory from other results of sociological research; and second, indirectly, by defining at the outset the functional features (i.e., specific expected applications or contributions) that distinguish a theory from other results of sociological research, and only later deriving its structural properties as the necessary prerequisites of expected functions. The choice of the method of explication is bound up with the position taken with respect to the relative importance of structural versus functional features in characterizing scientific results; what is more characteristic of scientific results, their internal makeup or their external uses?

I take the second stand, which may be called *instrumentalist* or *functionalist*. According to Meehan (1968) this position holds that,

> knowledge is only a tool or instrument, hence that it can be evaluated only in terms of its human uses—its value to man [p. 17].
>
> . . . The quality of knowledge depends on the purposes that it will serve [p. 18].
>
> . . . We can therefore distinguish the instruments by the needs they are capable of satisfying, or putting the matter another way, define the characteristics of the instrument according to the need it is intended to satisfy [p. 20].

The implication of these considerations for the present discussion is that one can not define the structure that a theory should have without previous determination of its expected functions.

Theoretical Function

What are the functions of scientific theories? What do we expect of them? What role do we ascribe to them? What needs are they supposed to satisfy?

Let us start from the more fundamental question, namely what are the functions of scientific results as such, all types of scientific results; that is, those sets or systems of propositions that are formulated as the end products of scientific research? What do we expect of them? What do we need them for? What roles do they play?

The most obvious answer would probably be that they contribute to our understanding of the world and to our mastery over the world. Let us make precise the meaning of this claim. To begin with the first aspect: What does it mean that the scientific results contribute to our understanding of the world? It means that they provide *answers to some questions about the world*. And as to the second aspect: What does it mean that scientific results contribute to our mastery over the world? The answer is not so simple. Obviously, it cannot mean that scientific results have any immediate influence on the phenomena or processes of reality. Such influence can be exerted only by material forces, among them human actions, but certainly not by linguistic entities like propositions or systems of propositions. These can provide only the particular intellectual support for human actions. And this support consists of directives for action—in other words, *answers to some questions* of the type, how should one act to attain certain goals? We arrive at the conclusion that all types of scientific results may be construed as the answers to some questions. As Harre observed in a similar vein: "A useful way of studying the methods of the sciences is to imagine them as means for answering certain kinds of questions about happenings [p. 3]." The types of possible questions determine the types of answers *and* the types of scientific results.

I suggest a fourfold typology of scientific questions and scientific answers. The first type consists of *factographic questions* in the standard form: "What is it like?" (Here one can also qualify some other variants: "Is this and this such and such?" "What is such and such?" "Which of those is such and such?") If a certain scientific result gives a satisfactory answer to a question of this type, I shall say that it performs a *descriptive function*.

The second type consists of *explanatory questions* in the standard form: "Why it is like this?" (Here one can also qualify some other variants. For example: "What is the reason for its being like this?" "What is its cause?" "For what purpose is it like this?") If a certain scientific result gives a satisfactory answer to a question of this type, I shall say that it performs an *explanatory function*.

The third type consists of prognostic questions in the standard form: "What will it be like?" (Here one can also qualify certain variants: "When will it be like this?" "Will it be like this at all?" "Which of those will be like this?" "What will be like this?") If a certain scientific result gives a satisfactory answer to a question of this type, I shall say that it performs a *prognostic function*.

The fourth type consists of *practical questions* in the standard form: "How to act in order for something to be like this?" (Here one can also qualify, for instance, variants such as: "What to abstain from in order for something to become like this?" "How to act in order for something not to become like this?") If a certain scientific result gives a satisfactory answer to a question of this type, I shall say that it performs a *practical function*.

Which of these questions and which of these functions is characteristic of a theory and only of a theory? Both in philosophy of science and in sociology, theory is usually assigned three functions. Bunge (1967, Vol, II: 2) argues that in empirical science, theories are built in order to explain, predict, and furnish support for planning or acting.

Similarly, in sociological literature, Jahoda, Deutsch, and Cook (1951: 337) are explicit on this point: "It is the function of theory to explain observations in such a way as to make prediction possible. This is a goal of practical as well as scientific significance." A. Malewski (1964) backed his case for theoretical sociology in like fashion: "The social scientist who refuses to restrict his findings to the statements of fact, and wishes to explain and predict them as well as to act effectively, requires theoretical knowledge [p. 1]." In sum, a theory is usually said to have three functions: explanatory, predictive, and practical. So far, only one item in our typology has been eliminated, namely descriptive function. There is widespread agreement on the atheoretical character of this function. The answers to descriptive questions are seen as making up the scientific descriptions, and descriptions are strictly distinguished from theories (see Ajdukiewicz 1965; Brodbeck 1969).

Nevertheless, we are still left with a rather indeterminate characterization of theory—and no structural properties of theory can be determined if we stay with this heterogeneous set of three functions. The way out of this difficulty is suggested by the question of whether all three functions are equally significant, or are some perhaps more significant than others. The question of primacy may be understood in at least two ways. First, primacy may be understood in *motivational terms*. Then, the question could be phrased in the following way: Which of these functions is taken into account as the ultimate justification of theoretical efforts? In various historical epochs, the answer could probably take various forms. In our times, the modern scientific ethos requires science to be closely linked with practice. This attitude is revealed when in practical decision making an increasing role is ascribed to research and expert opinion, as well as when practical applications are proposed as the foremost evaluative criteria of research results. Practice as scientific and science as practical are the two phrases that reflect the spirit of our epoch, and no less so of the social sciences (see Myrdal 1953). The ultimate justification of theoretical efforts is presently seen in the sphere of practical applications. This point is emphasized by Meehan (1968): "The aim of inquiry is to acquire some measure of control over a particular event or set of events [p. 19]."

Granted all this, the motivational sense of primacy is not of much use for our purposes. The practical applicability of a theory is obviously dependent on the content of theoretical propositions and not so much on their form. One cannot derive any specific formal or structural properties of a theory postulating its practical function as the basis of derivation. We must look for another sense of primacy.

Second, primacy may be understood in *pragmatic terms.* Then the question could be phrased: Which of the three functions constitutes the precondition for the realization of the other two; or, in different terms: Which of these functions is such, that if it were realized, the others could also be realized, at least potentially? To determine the primacy among the three possibilities it is sufficient to consider two pairs of alternatives: explanatory function versus predictive function, and explanatory function versus practical function.

It seems self-evident that if we possess an adequate explanation of a particular phenomenon, event, or process, i.e., if we know why it appears or its "mechanism," then we can also predict if and when it will appear. Of course this possibility is often only potential. Actually the formulation of specific prognosis may appear difficult or even impossible at a given moment, because in order to formulate it one must be furnished not only with the explanatory knowledge of the particular "mechanism," but also with the descriptive knowledge of the actual situation in all its relevant aspects. To put it otherwise, we must know not only the "mechanism" of the process, but also the initial state of affairs, in order to predict the future state. In sociology we very often lack the descriptive knowledge of this type, which is due in part to the tremendous number of variables involved, and in part to difficulties in determining the value of each variable itself. (This is a predicament which haunts natural sciences as well, at least some of the disciplines. The example most often quoted concerns meteorology, which is fully aware of all the principal "mechanisms" of atmospheric phenomena, and at the same time is not tremendously successful in weather forecasting, precisely because of the enormous number of variables that codetermine the specific baric situation, as well as the difficulty of determining their constantly changing values.) Nevertheless, all these difficulties are factual rather than necessary, and as such they do not invalidate my main point, that principally, or potentially, providing an explanation is a sufficient condition for successful prediction.

What about the reversal of this claim? Is it enough to predict successfully in order to understand the mechanism of events? Of course not. In everyday life we predict with certainty that the sun will rise in the morning, and that milk on the stove will boil over,

even if we have no idea of Keppler's laws or the principles of thermo-
dynamics. The same is often true of science. The majority of prognostic methods utilized in social sciences are precisely of this sort.
The extrapolations of present trends in demographic or economic
predictions, the technological forecasts based on the opinion of ex-
perts, so-called Delphic prognoses are often surprisingly adequate.
All this is not based on any explanatory knowledge as to the mechanisms of respective processes—such knowledge is still sought, and
yet we predict quite successfully. Thus, making a prediction is not
sufficient proof that there exists a suitable explanation. It follows
that with respect to the first pair of alternatives, explanatory function
must be considered as pragmatically primary to the predictive
function.

The confrontation of explanatory function and practical function
leads to a similar result. It seems self-evident that if we know the
mechanism of a certain phenomenon, event, or process, we can specify
what should be done in order to bring it into being, modify it, or
transform it. Again, this is only a potentiality. Actually, in order to
put our directives to use, we must also be furnished with the technological capabilities ("know-how" and not only "know-that"), as well
as capability to decide what we wish to do. Unfortunately, in sociology
we most often lack both. Even if we know what should be done,
we often do not know how to carry it out, and besides, even if we
had the requisite practical knowledge, our social status of a "powerless
elite" would probably preclude its implementation. Certain consolation
may be found in the fact that a similar situation obtains, for example,
in astronomy, geology, and genetics. However, as previously mentioned, these difficulties are factual and not necessary and as such
do not invalidate our point that principally, or potentially, providing
an explanation is a sufficient condition for successful practical action.
Meehan (1968) has argued similarly:

> An explanation is an instrument that suggests ways in which man
> might in principle intervene in an empirical situation to alter the course
> of events [p. 21].

> . . . To accept an explanation as valid means to believe that if it
> could be acted upon, events could be controlled in particular ways. . . .
> Knowledge of the way in which events come about makes it possible
> to intervene, in principle at least, to control them [p. 23].

And what about the reversal of this claim? Is it enough to act
successfully in order to understand the mechanism of events? Certainly

not. The most characteristic feature of everyday actions is again that they are devoid of explanatory basis. We manage somehow in thousands of practical situations, without the faintest idea of the relevant mechanisms rendering our actions successful. And the same is true of many branches of applied science. The majority of the so-called "sociotechniques," or directives of social engineering, are based on commonsense knowledge, intuition, folk wisdom, and are not rigorously derived from sociological or psychological explanation. The explanatory knowledge of the requisite sort is still sought, and at the same time successful action is, to some extent, the imperative of our survival. Thus, providing an effective directive for practical action is not necessarily a sign of deeper explanatory knowledge. It follows that with respect to the second pair of alternatives, explanatory function is again pragmatically primary to the practical function.

I have arrived at the conclusion that among the three functions usually ascribed to scientific theory, the primacy rests with the explanatory function. There is a consensus on this point among social scientists. Krech, Crutchfield, and Ballachey (1962) have emphasized that: "The major objective of science is not primarily to control and predict, but to understand. Effective control is a reward of understanding, and accuracy in prediction is a check on understanding [p. 2]." Berelson and Steiner (1964) have made the same point: "The scientist wants to know why and how, and to be able to prove it. If he can, then he can predict the conditions under which the specified behavior will occur. And if he can do that, then the question of control enters in as well [p. 17]." Recently, similar observations were made by Kaplan and Manners (1972): "Being able to predict correctly allows us to anticipate events and thus to prepare for them. But if we know why we are able to predict correctly, we are provided with a mechanism by which we may also be able to intervene in events and exert some control over them [p. 18]."

If the explanatory function of the theory is primary, then it is obviously best suited to be the basic element in the functional definition of a theory. Hence, I propose to understand a theory as *any scientific result that fulfills an explanatory function,* and such a result only. The structure of that particular result, i.e., the type of characteristic elementary propositions and the form of their interrelations, is to be considered as a necessary, logical consequence of explanatory function, or what amounts to the same, as a necessary prerequisite for fullfilling that particular function.

This sort of approach to defining a theory is not very common in the social sciences. But some hints pointing in this direction are certainly to be found in sociological literature. The functional definition of a theory by its explanatory function is suggested in several works of Homans. Defending the case for "Bringing Men Back In" the domain of sociological theory, he (Homans 1964) gives the following characterization of a theory as such: "The explanation of a phenomenon is the theory of the phenomenon. A theory is nothing—it is not a theory—unless it is an explanation [p. 811]." In another connection, Homans (1962) noted: "Men were not to be denied the right to ask the question 'Why?'; to ask for explanation. To answer the question was to find, if possible, the higher-order propositions from which, under specified given conditions, the empirical findings could be derived. To answer the question was therefore to construct a theory [p. 47]." Homans's *The Nature of Social Science* supplements this definition with a new and significant element. Homans seems to be aware of certain undesirable ramifications of his earlier claims. These are the tremendous multiplication and atomization of theories. If theory is rendered equivalent to an individual, singular explanation, then obviously we have as many theories as explanations, ergo as many theories as sociological phenomena perceived as problematic and approached with the question "Why?" To avoid this difficulty, Homans (1967) suggested applying the term *theory* not to "an explanation of a single phenomenon, but to a cluster of explanations of related phenomena, when the explanations, the deductive systems, share some of the same general propositions [p. 26]."

Functional definition of a theory may also be found in social anthropology. Manners and Kaplan (1968) observed:

> In this view, theories are generalizations or, more commonly, sets of interrelated generalizations, that explain facts, general statements and even other theories. To put it another way, theories are generalizations, but generalizations of a particular kind, namely, those which relate classes or types of phenomena to one another in certain determinate ways. . . . Theories, if they are any good should tell us why certain empirical generalizations or regularities of nature obtain. Thus all theories are framed to answer a "why" question [p. 7].

The intuitions inherent in the quoted characterizations of a theory are in my opinion extremely fruitful. But, unfortunately, none of the authors mentioned earlier develops them in any systematic manner or traces their implications on the structural level. Granted that every theory must perform an explanatory function, the most interesting question seems to be: How must a theory be constructed in order to perform this function effectively? To this question I shall address myself presently.

Theoretical Structure

According to the functional definition, theory is conceived as a set or system of propositions that explains certain phenomena, events, or processes, or answers the question "Why?" of those phenomena, events, or processes. Can any answer of this type be considered a theory? Of course not. The set or system of propositions making up an answer will have to satisfy certain criteria (both with respect to each proposition, and with respect to their ordering) before it will count as a theory. What are the criteria that allow us to distinguish a theory from other possible answers to the question "Why?" What are the structural requirements of a proper theoretical answer? To define these criteria is obviously equivalent to defining the structure of a theory.

The question "Why?" may be phrased in various contexts. Depending on several pragmatic circumstances having to do with the questioner, his intentions, the context in which the question is phrased, etc., the criteria of a satisfactory or adequate answer will vary. As Brown (1963) remarked: ". . . giving of an explanation always takes place in a context. . . . It is the context of the question that determines what will count as an explanatory answer [p. 159]."

In everyday situations we readily accept an answer which satisfies our intellectual curiosity, i.e., reduces the state of doubt or uncertainty that stimulated us to question in the first place. Obviously, this is a subjective and highly relative criterion of adequacy. Besides, the criterion is very liberal; it allows us to treat as explanation a very diversified set of answers. Brodbeck (1969) is right that there are "as many senses of explain as there are possible answers in common speech to the question Why? [p. 366]." For example, if the question concerns some form of human behavior, say it is phrased: "Why has John gotten married?" any of the following, quite diverse answers could appear satisfactory in the everyday discourse. First, the answer may refer to the genesis of the event; that is, the chain of events preceding it and supposedly connected causally with the event in question (e.g., "They have been going steady for two years"). Second, the answer may refer to some emotional motivations accompanying the event (e.g., "He fell in love with her"). Third, it may refer to some rational motivations accompanying the event (e.g., "Her father is a millionaire"). Fourth, it may refer to some psychological disposi- tions or traits of the persons involved (e.g., "He always fell in love very easily"). Fifth, it may refer to some objective constraints which in a given situation could not have been possibly resisted (e.g., "She forced him to marry her"). Sixth, it may refer to some general trend or regularity (e.g., "Everybody is marrying very early these days"). Certainly the list is not complete; many other answers could qualify as everyday, common-sense explanations.

Is the subjective, liberal, relative psychological criterion of intellec- tual satisfaction a sufficient scientific answer? The essential, defining properties of science entail negative answers. In a scientific context we do not search for the criteria of relevance or validity in the realm of common-sense usage, but rather attempt to disentangle scientific assertions from any considerations of a pragmatic or subjective charac- ter and define some intersubjective and absolute measures of their adequacy. It means that in the case of explanations we must be able to appraise them intrinsically, with no regard for the particular persons who formulate them, their motives or intentions, particular circum- stances in which they were formulating an explanation, etc. As Brod- beck (1969) remarked: "The task is to show what, so to speak, in the facts themselves, or, to be accurate, in the statements asserting them, rather than in the mind or behavior of a particular person or group of persons, makes one or more statements a reason, in a precise logical sense of reason, for one or more others [p. 370]."

A scientifically satisfactory answer to the question "Why?" consists in the indication that the fact or regularity being explained fits into the scientific picture of the world, accepted at a given time–or in other terms, that the proposition describing that fact or regularity is not contradicted by any propositions in the accepted body of scien- tific knowledge, but rather conversely, it is entailed by some of those propositions. The same point is made by Hempel (1965) in arguing that the understanding conveyed by the explanation is due to the "insight that the explanadum fits into, or can be subsumed under, a system of uniformities represented by empirical laws or theoretical principles [p. 488]." Such and only such an explanation that satisfies the above criterion will be referred to as a *scientific explanation*.

But obviously, every scientific explanation will not by the same token qualify as a theory. The explanatory question "Why *q*?" is answered in the scientific context: "*q* because *p*." It seems that several additional criteria referring both to *q* (i.e., the explained proposition or explanandum), to *p* (i.e., the explaining propositions or explanans), and also to the relationship between them conveyed by the word *because* must be satisfied before we can speak of a full-fledged theory. Therefore, by theory I shall mean only a particularly qualified answer to the question "Why?" I propose to consider seven additional requirements, each of which is necessary and all of which in conjunction make up the total sufficient condition of an adequate theory.

Specification of Explanandum

The first requirement refers to the propositions that are to be explained. The explanandum of a theory must be specified, which entails three partial requirements. First, one must specify the *object* of the question "Why?"—the concrete domain that is to be explained by a theory. However, one cannot meaningfully ask the question "Why?" of an object. For example, one cannot ask: "Why society?" "Why a social group?" "Why an individual?" Further specification is needed which concerns the *problem* of the theory.

To specify the problem of a theory, one must name, in the first place, the particular properties that are predicated of a given object. The question, "Why has a given object this or that property?" is no longer meaningless. For example, one may ask: "Why is Polish society integrated?" "Why is a boy scout troop highly effective in carrying out group goals?" "Why do people who have been socially repressed display aggressive attitudes and why are they particularly apt to be racially prejudiced?"

In certain cases, in order to specify the problem one must specify not only the particular property that is ascribed to a given object, but also the scope of the ascription; that is, one must determine whether the property in question applies to a singular object, some selected cases in a given class, or all objects in that class. The theoretical problem is fully specified only when both the property and its scope are unambiguously defined. When the two partial requirements discussed here are met, we know what our theoretical question refers to and what it predicates. But we do not yet know if the specified object is in fact characterized by the specified property. To put it briefly, we do not know whether the assumption of the question is true or false and, consequently, whether the theoretical problem is real or apparent. Thus, the third requirement entails the empirical substantiation, or *justification*, of the explanandum. To follow my examples, one must determine empirically whether Polish society is in fact integrated or not, whether a boy scout troop is in fact effective in attaining group goals, and whether repressed individuals really display aggressive attitudes and racial prejudice.

One cannot help reflecting that the three fundamental steps in the construction of a scientific theory, which were briefly characterized in this section, are often neglected in sociological inquiry, and as a result we encounter time and again many explanations of pseudo-facts that were never carefully checked in the first place.

Validity of Explanation

The second major requirement refers to the relationship between the propositions that are explained (*explanandum*) and the propositions that are explaining (*explanans*). There must exist a certain determinate link between them in order for the whole explanation to be valid. This link is usually conceived in logical terms as the relation of entailment or derivation, either of deductive or probabilistic character. Explanans must either imply explanandum in a strict, deductive sense, i.e., the truth of explaining propositions must make the truth of the explained proposition logically, analytically certain, or at least the explanans must imply the explanandum in a weaker, probabilistic sense; that is, the truth of the explaining propositions must provide a strong inductive support for the explained proposition, or, less precisely, it must make the explained proposition highly probable. Manners and Kaplan (1968) phrased this requirement in the following way:

> We take the position that factual statements or empirical generalizations are explained when it is shown that they can be subsumed under a set of theoretical statements, either by being derived from such statements in formal, deductive fashion, or when the connection between the theoretical statements and the generalizations and facts is probabilistic one [p. 8].

This is basically congruent with the classical scheme of scientific explanation widely accepted in contemporary philosophy of science and elaborated most extensively by Hempel (1965). According to the "covering-law model," a scientific explanation is a particular argument that "accounts for a given phenomenon by subsuming it under laws; i.e., by showing that its occurrence could have been inferred— either deductively or with a high probability—by applying certain laws of universal or of statistical form to specified antecedent circumstances [p. 302]." The same logic applies to the explanation of regularities or laws themselves.

Therefore, an answer to the question "Why?" may be considered as a valid explanation if and only if the content of the question (or to put it more precisely, the assumption of the question—that which the question asserts) is the consequence, in either of the defined meanings, of the content of the answer (of that which the answer asserts). For example, if the question were "Why is this group highly cohesive?" and the answer, "Because it is engaged in external conflict, and every group engaged in external conflict is highly cohesive," then the explanation as a whole would be valid. The explanandum is implied by the explanans by virtue of the modus ponens rule of deductive logic.

Note that the validity of the explanation does not presuppose the actual truth values of particular propositions. It refers solely to the link between them. If this link obtains, the explanation is valid even if all component propositions are false. The explanation that is valid but whose component propositions have indeterminate truth value is sometimes referred to as a potential explanation. To transform it into an actual, full-fledged explanation, some additional requirements must be satisfied referring to the explaining propositions themselves.

Testability of Explanans

The third requirement refers to the propositions included in the explanans. They must have empirical meaning or, in other terms, they must be potentially testable; that is, there must exist a definite possibility of their direct verification or falsification, or at least indirect confirmation or refutation. The answer to the question "Why?" is testable if one can point out the effective method by which it may be found whether it is true or not, in the finished sequence of experimental or experiential operations.

For example, if the question is, "Why does John usually conform to group norms?" and the answer, "Because he is intelligent and all intelligent people are conformists," this is clearly a testable answer, though hopefully false. We may directly verify whether John is intelligent or not by administering an intelligence test. We may also indirectly confirm the generalization to the effect that all intelligent people are conformists, by deriving its testable consequences—by deducing what facts had to obtain if it were true and checking whether these facts do obtain or not. One testable consequence would say, for example, that people scoring highest on an intelligence test (geniuses) should be expected to overconform. The historical evidence of Galileo, Giordano Bruno, and Copernicus, to name the first who come to mind, would falsify it immediately, and thus indirectly refute the generalization itself.

An explanation that is potentially testable, though not yet effectively tested, is sometimes referred to as a hypothetical explanation.

Justification of Explanans

The fourth requirement demands somewhat more of the propositions included in the explanans. They must not only be testable, but actually tested; in other words, they must have undergone a testing procedure whose results were positive. If this is the case, the propositions are directly verified or at least indirectly confirmed, and the complete answer to the question "Why?" may be considered justified.

For example, given the question, "Why are highly prestigeous group members most sensitive to group pressure?" and given the answer, "Because the higher the individual's rank in the group, the more interactions link him with other members of the group, and the more interactions he is involved in, the greater his sensitivity to group pressure" (see Homans 1950), the answer is justified because both generalizations have actually been confirmed in empirical research.

The explanation that has been tested and verified or confirmed may be referred to as a grounded explanation.

Pragmatic Completeness of Explanans

The fifth requirement refers to the specific content of the explaining propositions. The answer to the question "Why?" must be complete; it must not create new problems of an explanatory nature in place of the solved ones. This condition is met when none of the propositions included in explanans can be transformed into the assumption of the new "Why?" question, or when none of the explaining propositions can be considered problematic.

It is easily seen that this requirement is relativistic in at least three respects. First, it is relative to the subjective cognitive potential of an individual scholar. Something that is a given, unexplained datum for one may be further explained by another. Second, it is relative to the cognitive potential of a given discipline at a given point in its development. Something that today is considered a given, unexplainable datum may be explained tomorrow; likewise something that is considered a given, unexplainable datum in the context of one discipline may well be further explained by another discipline. Homans (1967) made this point quite explicitly: "As we move toward more and more general propositions, we reach, at any given time in the history of science, propositions that cannot themselves be explained. If we can judge from experience, this condition, for any particular proposition, is unlikely to last forever [p. 26]." And third, the criterion is also relative to the specific problem that inspired the theory construction. Something that can be justifiably considered a given, unexplainable datum from the point of view of one problem may well be in need of further explanation in terms of another problem (cf. Quine and Ullian 1970: 74).

Suppose that in answer to the question, "Why do the members of this group conform to the group's norms?" one were presented with the following propositions: "Social control in this group is effective, and wherever social control is effective, group members behave in a conforming manner." This answer, even if valid, testable, and justified is obviously not complete. The question "Why?" may be asked of both propositions included in the explanans. One may simply inquire: "Well, but why is social control effective in this particular group if it is ineffective in many others, and why should individuals behave conformingly if social control is effective." (To put it a little differently, what does social control have to do with conformist behavior, or what is the linking mechanism between the operation of social control and the behavior of people.) Following this course and persistently asking the question "Why?" of any propositions that were previously adduced as explanatory, one shall arrive at a point where an answer simply cannot be given (by him, by his discipline, or by the science of his epoch). Or, if the answer could be given, it would be irrelevant in terms of the initial problem. Such and only such an ultimate answer, consisting of the sequence of answers given on the way, may be considered as pragmatically complete.

What is the logical structure of a pragmatically complete explanation? It is a *system of explanations* that are linked in a specific manner. Namely, those propositions that have the status of being explaining propositions (explanans) in a certain explanation have simultaneously the status of explained ones (explanandum) in another explanation, and this obtains for all explanations in the system with the exception of the first and the last. The notion of a system of explanations, which is crucial for our further discussion, is precisely defined by Nikitin (1970):

> By a system of explanations I understand a set W of explanations which satisfies the following criteria: (a) it consists of more than one explanation, (b) for every explanation W_1 in this set, there is at least one explanation W_2 such that either one of the components of explanans of W_1 is also an explanandum of W_2, or an explanandum of W_1 is also one of the components of explanans of W_2, and (c) all the explanations in the set W are connected in a unified logical structure, which allows to move from one to the other by means of a finite sequence of logical operations [p. 242].

In somewhat metaphorical terms, the system of explanations is like a pyramid which consists of several layers of explanations built one over the other. The bottom of the pyramid is made up of the problematic assertions, and its provisional top is made up of the statements that for a certain reason are considered the ultimate answer at least for the time being.

I propose to call this type of propositional structure a *theory*. To repeat, I define theory as a system of scientific explanations in the sense specified in this discussion. I consider the construction of systems of explanations as the fundamental imperative of the further development of sociology, as a prerequisite for scientific maturity in our discipline. Nikitin (1970) argued forcefully that: "In the early descriptive and empirical phase in the history of science, the explanations, if constructed at all, have usually isolated, diffuse character. And conversely, the mature and theoretical phase is marked by the construction of explanatory systems [p. 252]." It seems indeed time for sociology to enter the second phase of its history.

An explanation that is scientific, specified, valid, testable, justified, and complete is here referred to as a theory. Yet, theory still may be inadequate. Some additional requirements of theoretical adequacy must be specified. One refers to the internal structure of the theory (its components and their interrelations), the other, to its external structure (the place in wider propositional wholes).

Semantic Consistency of the Theory

The sixth requirement refers to the language in which the explanations are phrased. More specifically, it refers to the variable and non-variable properties mentioned in the propositions of a theory, or in different terms, to the predicates of the theory.

The set of all the predicates appearing in the theory must be homogeneous and limited. The first partial requirement is referred to as the condition of semantic homogeneity. This condition is met by a theory which in the whole sequence of explanations built one over another consistently introduces the variable or nonvariable properties of the same type; e.g., sociological predicates only, psychological predicates only, or even predicates defined in terms of some particular orientation—holistic predicates only, individualistic predicates only, etc. A theory introducing both group integration and the intelligence quotient as its explanatory predicates would be obviously heterogenous. The same would be true of a theory mentioning both the threshold value of a stimulus and the force of the ego in its explanatory propositions. However, one must be aware of the approximate and somewhat ambiguous nature of this criterion and, consequently, apply it with care. This point is well made by Bunge (1967, Vol I: 393) who argued that there are some border cases wherein the decision on the semantic homogeneity of a theory may be very difficult. He points to theories in biochemistry or social psychology which were made possible by devising a new conceptual apparatus that unified seemingly disparate semantic families. The second partial requirement is referred to as the condition of semantic closure. It is met by a theory that introduces a restricted number of predicates into its propositions and avoids the opportunistic (ad hoc) addition of new variable or nonvariable properties to this set.

Unification of a Theory

The seventh and last requirement refers to the place of a given theory in the wider context of scientific knowledge. The theory should not be isolated, but rather linked with other theories in the more comprehensive theoretical system. What is the character of possible intertheoretical links? First, two or more theories may be formulated as answers to the same question; in other words, they may possess a common explanandum and different explanatory propositions. Each theory explains somewhat different aspects of the problem, approaches it from a somewhat different point of view, and all add up to a more comprehensive answer. For example, the theory of social control explains some aspects of conformist behavior from a sociological viewpoint, and the theory of the conforming personality explains other aspects of conformist behavior from a psychological point of view. This type of unification, where theories are linked by virtue of a common explanandum, may be called downward unification. To use a metaphor, several theoretical pyramids are here built on the common foundation.

Second, two or more theories may be formulated in the same way, but answer different questions; that is, they may possess a common explanans but different explained propositions. Each theory explains different problems, but all invoke the same explanatory principles. For instance, the hypothesis of frustration–aggression may be invoked as an ultimate explanatory proposition in theories of individual delinquency, as well as in the theories of war, prejudice, intergroup conflict, discrimination, etc. This type of unification, in which theories are linked by virtue of common explanans, may be referred to as upward unification: In metaphorical terms, several theoretical pyramids are here suspended under a common ceiling.

Our discussion in this chapter has led to some metascientific conclusions. If by a *theoretical structure* of a given discipline we shall understand the totality of propositions specified in the process of answering "why questions," then the above considerations entail a particular image of theoretical structure. It is conceived as a three-level hierarchy. In the words of Kemeny (1959): "We get a hierarchy of explanations, where the facts at the lowest level are explained by theories, and then each theory in turn is explained by the theories on a higher level, until we reach the limits of our present knowledge [p. 16]." On the first level we encounter singular explanations, linking in a systematizing structure some isolated propositions. On the second level we encounter singular theories, linking in a more comprehensive systematizing structure some isolated explanations. And on the third level we encounter theoretical systems unifying in the coherent whole a set of isolated theories. This image of the theoretical structure of science will guide my further analysis.

Chapter 3

THE NOTION OF
A CONCEPTUAL MODEL

The course of my argument thus far may be summarized as follows. First, I asked what is the primary function of a scientific theory. The answer was that it is to explain the facts of our experience. Second, I asked what structure must a scientific theory assume if it is to perform this function adequately. It was proposed that in order to explain adequately the facts of our experience, a theory must take the form of an explanatory system which is semantically consistent and unified. In this chapter I propose to follow the logic of the argument one step backward and ask what are the prerequisites for formulating a theory understood in this sense.

Certainly an adequate theory has many prerequisites. Each of the seven requirements specified in Chapter 2 obviously implies certain prerequisites. For example in order to satisfy the *syntactic require-ment* of validity, one must possess a set of inference rules allowing the deductive or probabilistic derivation of the explanandum from the explanans (or what amounts to the same—the subsumption of expla-nandum under explanans). In the simplest cases these rules are pro-vided by propositional logic (natural deduction) and by the calculus of probability (in the case of "inductive–statistical explanations"). In more complex cases, some more sophisticated mathematical calculi may appear necessary. In turn, to satisfy the *empirical requirements* of testability and justification, one must possess a set of empirical techniques (experimental or observational) allowing for the objective determination of whether a given object or class of objects is in fact characterized by a given property. Multiple volumes devoted to the techniques of sociological research, as well as to extensive criticism of such techniques, testify all too convincingly that this is a much more complex issue than would appear at first sight.

But I shall deal here neither with syntactic nor empirical prerequisites of sociological theory. Instead, I propose to focus our attention on the third group of requirements and, consequently, on the third set of prerequisites. They are the specification of the explanandum and the semantic consistency of the explanans, which may both be regarded as *semantic requirements*. These requirements have to do with the properties of a scientific language in which both major parts of the theory (explanandum, or that which the theory explains, and explanans, or that by which the theory explains) are to be expressed. To satisfy both requirements, obviously one must possess some sort of conceptual apparatus. What is this conceptual apparatus? On this point, present methodology and philosophy of social sciences have very little to say.

Admittedly, there is widespread recognition of the crucial significance of a conceptual apparatus with the help of which one defines, describes, and explains certain problematic matters. But this recognition rarely amounts to anything more than lip service. There is an amazing profusion of terms referring to this prerequisite of sociological theory. A casual review of current sociological literature reveals no less than 33 terms signifying one and the same metascientific concept. Thus, one encounters frame of reference (Zetterberg 1954; Parsons 1964; Ackerman and Parsons 1966); conceptual framework (Agassi 1960); theoretical framework and analytical approach (Hage 1972); analytical model (Hagen 1961); analytical system (Shanin 1972); analytical theory (Fallding 1968); ideal system (Lopreato 1971); scheme of interpretation and classification scheme (Schrag 1967); set of analytic categories and nonoperating definitions (Homans 1967); orienting statements (Homans 1967); definitional scheme and lines of conceptual abstraction (Smelser 1969); theoretical scheme (Blau 1969); theoretical orientation (Hage 1972; Manners and Kaplan 1968); theoretical guideline (Parsons 1964); general sociological orientation (Merton 1967); theoretical approach and methodological approach (Boskoff 1969); model (Beshers 1957); theoretical model (Bunge 1967); orienting model (Parsons 1964); conceptual model

(Sztompka 1968); paradigm, formal paradigm, theoretical perspective, scientific perspective, and conceptual picture (Bunge 1967); image of reality (Rose 1967); cognitive set (Taylor 1970; Rapoport 1967); and cognitive map (Ackerman and Parsons 1966).

A critical analysis of the meanings ascribed each term by these authors would require a separate volume. So, I must move directly to the more constructive explication of the involved notion. First, however, let me set forth my own terminological convention. From among the incredible array of terms listed above I choose two—to be used interchangeably: conceptual model and frame of reference. For reasons of brevity, I shall sometimes speak of a model or a frame but it should be remembered that I have only *conceptual model* in mind, not any other sense of this much-abused term (cf. Sztompka 1968).

In the explication of the notion of conceptual model I shall follow the same instrumentalist or functionalist strategy as previously. Therefore, in the first place I shall discuss the functions of a conceptual model relative to both semantic requirements of adequate theory. Later I shall briefly characterize the internal structure of a conceptual model, which seems a requisite for performing this function.

The Functions of a Conceptual Model

The first semantic requirement refers to the explanandum of the theory and calls for its specification. According to the notion of a theory proposed in Chapter 2, the initial explanandum of a theory consists of the assertion of fact (in the case of sociological theory, sociological fact). This assertion is phrased in the form of a so-called propositional statement, ascribing a certain predicate to a certain object. Thus, in the propositional statement, "The U.S. army is rigidly stratified," *U.S. army* may be considered the object and *stratified* as a predicate. Similarly, in the propositional statement, "Blacks in the United States have limited occupational opportunities," *blacks in the United States* may be considered the object and *limited occupational opportunities* the predicate.

It is clear that objects of a propositional statement may be of various types. One may distinguish two sorts of facts or, more precisely, two sorts of factual assertions: first, individual facts—the object refers to a singular entity (e.g., the U.S. army) and a certain property is predicated of this entity as a whole; second, generalized facts, or empirical generalizations—the object refers to a closed class of entities (say, blacks in the United States) and certain properties are predicated of each of the members of the class.

In a sociological context one may encounter both types of facts: individual and generalized. But it is worth noticing that only some specific subtype of individual facts is usually considered problematic in sociology. Usually, in a sociological context, we do not account for facts such as "John is aggressive," or "Mary gave in to the demands of the group," which refer to individual human beings or individual human acts. Rather, we focus on the facts in which the object refers to certain societal wholes: social groups, societies, communities, comprehensive social processes, etc. These societal wholes are traditionally spoken of as realities sui generis, emergent entities that are not equivalent to the simple sums of their elements (people, minor social changes). They are characterized by means of specific global predicates, which cannot be meaningfully ascribed to the elements; for instance, integration, cohesion, stratification, institutionalization, etc., in the case of social groupings, and directiveness, progressiveness, and cyclical character in the case of social processes. Obviously, these global predicates are formed by a certain transformation of our knowledge about elements and their interrelations; therefore, facts of this type, though apparently singular, may ultimately be considered as generalizations. The second type of facts, generalizations par excellence, refer not to social wholes, but to social aggregates, sets of individuals characterized by means of elementary predicates ascribed to each of the individuals separately. As Brown (1963) observed: "In the social sciences, as in other sciences, individual actions—those of a given person—are usually interesting only as members of a class of actions. It is the class of actions which is to be explained, not merely the actions of one of the class members [p. 73]." A similar point was made by Harre (1968): "In prescientific explanations . . . what we seek to explain are particular happenings . . . [p. 30]." On the other hand, according to Harre (1968: 30) the characteristic of mature science is "the giving of general explanations in which we seek to explain not a single particular happening but a class of happenings. . . ."

It seems that in order to specify the explanandum of a theory we must specify a certain sociological fact, usually of a generalized type. The view that sociological facts are given, are somewhere "out there" waiting to be discovered, is appealing in its simplicity, but totally and fundamentally mistaken. Reality itself is infinitely complex, multi-dimensional, continuous, and fluid. And, given human limitations, "If we are to be able to talk about something, we must be able to see it as a limited subject matter. We must be able to say what falls within the subject matter and what without, in order to see what kind of questions can profitably be asked [Emmet 1958: 12]." In short, we must "slice the cake" of experience in a specific manner, take some elements, some aspects, or some dimensions into considera-tion, and disregard or exclude others. What fragment of reality ac-quires the rank of a fact depends to a large extent on how the cake is sliced. We do not discover facts that are given, we construct them out of reality with the help of our particular tools. Facts are not merely encountered, they are produced. The quality of the sculpture depends as much on the type of marble as on the skills of the sculptor and the sharpness of his chisel. In the case of a scientific theory, the tools are a little different; they are conceptual. We filter our experience through the screen of our conceptual apparatus and, as a result, we transform it into scientific constructs, and, of course, scientific facts.

These points have been argued very cogently by Ackerman and Parsons (1966):

> Sociology is not a tabula rasa upon which things called "facts" inscribe their determinate and essential paths and shapes. . . . We approach our data as humans; and, as humans, we approach with differential receptivity and intentionality everything toward which we propose cogni-tive orientation. . . . Data do not simply impose their structure on our inquiring and open minds; we interact with "facts." . . . There is a formative input to analysis, the components of which are not born ex nihilo in or of the moment of encounter with "facts"; rather, they are grounded in the orientation and frame of reference of the analyst. Indeed in major part we create, we do not merely encounter, facticity [p. 24].

I shall attempt to grasp the essence of this conceptual input inherent in every sociological analysis through the notion of a conceptual model or a frame of reference. Thus, without now specifying this notion, it might be said that a determinate conceptual model is a necessary prerequisite for specifying the explanandum of sociological theory.

The second semantic requirement refers to the explanans of the theory and calls for its semantic consistency. According to our notion of a theory, the ultimate explanans consists of multiple propositions bound in small systematic clusters of singular explanations, and built hierarchically one over the other. These propositions are of two types. Some of them are factual assertions referring to certain facts, different from those that are to be explained. And some of them are lawlike assertions, positing a regular relationship between facts, typically in the form of conditional statements to the effect that if a certain fact obtains, then some other facts will also be true (either unexceptionally, or with a high degree of statistical probability). Thus, in case of both types of propositions, their essential elements are made up of sociological facts. To require that the explanans be semantically consistent is, therefore, tantamount to requiring the semantical consistency of facts. What does the semantic consistency of facts signify?

It cannot possibly mean that all facts should be identical in content. This would preclude any derivation and, by the same token, any explanation and any theory. The facts must be heterogeneous, but they must have something in common. Since that something cannot be derived from the substantive content of facts, it can be derived only from the conceptual input of the theoretician. In short, all facts must be constructed in terms of the same conceptual model.

Yet this is not the whole story. The conceptual model informing the propositions of the explanans must not only be common to all of these propositions, but it must also be identical with the model that has been applied in formulating the explanandum of the same theory. This additional requirement is emphasized in a somewhat different connection by Taylor (1970). Among the essential questions that allow the evaluation of any theoretical statement, he mentioned the following:

> Are variables linked in a proposition defined on the same unit? If the answer to this question is no, it indicates that a logical error has been committed that ordinarily will lead to a great deal of confusion. . . . For example a proposition may link a variable defined on an individual with a variable defined on a group [p. 174].

The same applies ceteris paribus to whole propositions and also to more comprehensive propositional structures linked in a theory. If the explanans is defined in terms of a different conceptual scheme from the explanandum, then the same logical error invalidates whole theory, not only the singular proposition.

Thus, both semantic requirements of an adequate theory appear to be reducible to one and the same demand; before attempting the construction of a system of explanations, one must specify the conceptual model or frame of reference and stick to this model very carefully throughout the whole process of theory construction—both in specifying the initial explanandum and in formulating the explanatory propositions on all levels of theoretical structure. *A conceptual model is a necessary prerequisite of theory construction.*

Let us clarify the notion of a conceptual model, beginning with its functions and deriving some conclusions as to its structure. Generally speaking, the basic function of a conceptual model is to organize experience. This is achieved by a twofold process. First, a conceptual model selects a certain region of experience, defines the boundaries of that region, and in this way determines what is taken into consideration and what is dismissed as irrelevant. "We exclude—and what we exclude haunts us at the walls we set up. We include—and what we include limps, wounded by amputation. And most importantly, we must live with all this, we must live with our wounded and our ghosts [Ackerman and Parsons 1966: 26]." In a more down-to-earth way, the same function of a conceptual model was discussed by Shanin (1972): "The many-sided character of reality renders any analysis a necessarily partial image of some selected aspects, a fewer-dimensional picture of a multi-dimensional object [p. 361]." A conceptual model contributes to solving the "boundary problem" that arises in any theoretical inquiry.

Second, a conceptual model identifies loci of significant variables within a selected region of experience; it defines the dimensions of possible variability within the boundaries, and in this way gives a certain direction to the theoretical propositions. This function of a conceptual model is emphasized by Smelser (1969): "Without a conceptual framework, it is not possible to identify ranges of empirical variation that are scientifically problematical [p. 3]." In the same vein, Ackerman and Parsons (1966) argued that the conceptual model "directs the attention of the analyst to relevant questions and to the loci of relevant problems [pp. 39–40]." And Merton (1967) noted that they provide "general orientation toward data suggesting types of variables which theories must somehow take into account [p. 52]." In this way, a conceptual model contributes to the solution of the "locus problem" appearing in any theoretical inquiry.

We may sum up the functional characterization of a conceptual model with the explicitly *functional definition* suggested by Emmet (1958): "By model is here meant a way of representing a complex of relationships the adoption of which affects how the subject is approached [p. 45]."

The Structure of a Conceptual Model

But the characterization of a conceptual model cannot stop at this point. We are led to ask what is the necessary structure of a model, the prerequisite for fulfilling the functions ascribed to the model in the preceding section. A conceptual model is not equivalent to a set of analytic categories or to the simple enumeration of concepts. It is not a vocabulary for speaking about certain objects, but rather a unified image of those objects. It is a complex construct made up of assumptions referring to some selected domain of reality and characterizing it in a simplified or idealized manner. In the words of Lopreato (1971), it is conceived as "a construct and an assumption the scientist makes about the actual order within a given phenomenon in terms of the interdependencies existing among those factors that are deemed crucial for that order [p. 310]." Or, again, in Hagen's (1961) terms, it is "a mental construct consisting of a set of elements in interrelation, the elements and their interrelations being precisely defined [p. 144]."

According to the criterion of generality, two sets of assumptions can be distinguished analytically within any conceptual model. The first set consists of *general assumptions* defining the basic outline or framework of the given image of reality. In the sociological context, assumptions of this type will answer such questions as: "Is society something real, or is it only a denomination for a bundle of heterogeneous phenomena, events, or processes?" "Is it a system or a simple aggregation of elements?" "Is it organismlike or mechanismlike?" "Is it changing in a random manner or directively and regularly?" Each of the general assumptions opens up certain possibilities for conceptualizing the model's internal structure; each allows for certain structural alternatives within a given framework or creates certain dimensions of possible internal variability within the model.

These possibilities are realized by the second set of assumptions, the *particular assumptions* of the conceptual model. They define concrete choices along each of the dimensions of variability; they decide on one possible polar alternative rather than the other. In a sociological context, particular assumptions will answer such questions as: "Are societal elements mutually dependent or autonomous?" "Are the relationships between the elements ordinarily harmonious or, rather, antagonistic?" "Is society tending toward equilibrium or toward disruption?" "Is social change usually endogenous or exogenous?"

A fully specified conceptual model must include both sets of assumptions. If specified, a conceptual model provides a definite "property space" within which theoretical propositions for explanatory structures may be meaningfully formulated. It generates a language for theory construction. There is a limited number of concepts which are meaningful in the frame of a given model. Some concepts denote the constant, general properties of the given domain of reality. They constitute the *basic language* of a given theory. Some other concepts denote the particular properties (variables) that may be displayed by phenomena within this domain. They constitute the *specific language* of a given theory. These and only these concepts should be applied in the subsequent process of theory construction.

We may sum up our discussion by suggesting the following *structural definition:* A conceptual model is a set of assumptions defining both the general, constant characteristics and the possible range of the particular, variable characteristics of a given domain of reality.

In view of the preceding discussion, the specification of a conceptual model obviously must precede theory construction proper; i.e., the positing of contingent, empirical propositions and the organizing of them in an explanatory hierarchy. Therefore, in a sense, a conceptual model has a priori flavor. But it does not necessarily follow that it is totally arbitrary. There exists a precise criterion—the instrumentalist criterion—whereby some models are deemed adequate and others inadequate. The conceptual model is conceived here as a tool or an instrument of theory construction. And as with all tools, "by their fruit you shall judge them." A conceptual model can be judged only in terms of its fecundity, in view of the theory or theories it generates. If the theory phrased in terms of the model is well confirmed, the model receives equally good justification and must be considered adequate. And if the theory phrased in terms of the model is refuted, the model must be considered inadequate. Needless to say, a model that is built for its own sake with no progeny in view is devoid of any justification whatsoever, and must be judged as totally sterile.

In Part II, I attempt to reconstruct and appraise a conceptual model that seems most fruitful and promising for the generation of sociological theory.

SYSTEMIC–FUNCTIONAL MODELS
Substantive Continuities in Sociological Theory

Chapter 4

1882723

FUNCTIONALISM IN SOCIOLOGY AND SOCIAL ANTHROPOLOGY

This study is not concerned with the history of sociological ideas. But to set the field for our proper analytic inquiry it is necessary to review some milestones in the long debate over the functional orientation in sociology and social anthropology. It will give us a tentative outline of the body of thought which will be examined in the course of this volume. In this body of thought we shall seek the components of a conceptual model for the construction of a general theory of society.

The basic tenets of functional orientation were laid down in the 1920s by the Polish-born anthropologist Bronislaw Malinowski and the British anthropologist A. R. Radcliffe-Brown. Studying primitive tribal communities in the Pacific islands (Trobriand and Andaman, respectively), they found that the prevailing evolutionistic or diffusionistic approach was basically inadequate and they suggested a new orientation. It consisted of analyzing the primitive communities as ongoing systemic wholes, looking for interrelations of elements within them and the mechanisms through which each of the elements contributed to the satisfaction of some presumed needs of the people or some more abstract societal requisites. In place of a traditional question, "How did the given institution, behavior pattern, norm, value, etc., come about?" they substituted the question, "What is its present role, how does it fit into the context of a wider social whole?" This reversal of perspective proved extremely fruitful for empirical field research. The functional orientation came to dominate social anthropology and today is very important in the discipline (among the most outstanding representatives of modern functionalism in anthropology are E. E. Evans-Pritchard, A. Richards, S. F. Nadel, R. Firth, R. Piddington, and many others).

The prominence of the functional orientation in anthropology brought it to the attention of sociologists, who attempted to apply a similar approach to the study of modern, complex, and differentiated societies. It was in the post–World War II period that the sociological impact of functionalism was felt most strongly. In 1945, K. Davis and W. E. Moore wrote a short article of unexpected importance in the history of sociology. They tried to apply the functional perspective to a central sociological issue: social stratification. Four years later, R. K. Merton (1949) codified some methodological and conceptual problems of functional analysis in a famous paradigm and presented certain substantive results of theory construction following a functional approach. In the fifties, the functional "school" in sociology acquired its identity, as well as its prophet in Talcott Parsons. The development of functional conceptual schemes for social analysis was furthered by M. Levy, E. Shils, N. Smelser, R. Bales, Ph. Selznick, D. Easton, D. E. Apter, K. Deutsch, G. E. Almond, and many others.

The debate over functionalism has been going on for almost half a century. Martindale (1965) is correct that "Most primary theoretical and methodological debates in post war social science have centered on functionalism and alternatives to it [p. ix]." The assessment of functionalism ranges from total acceptance to total rejection, but strangely enough, the basic question, "What is functionalism and what is its scientific value for present-day sociology?" remains unanswered.

It seems to me that the difficulty with most evaluations of functionalism is precisely that they are total. In the course of its prolonged and complex development, functionalism became an extremely differentiated, heterogeneous corpus of thought. As Nagel (1961) aptly observed: "The label of functionalism covers a variety of distinct (though in some cases, closely related) conceptions [p. 522]." To evaluate it, one must be very precise as to the aspect, or dimension, of functionalist thought being discussed. Any worthwhile critique must be particular, individualized, taking each aspect or dimension separately. For the purpose of such a critique, I think it possible to distinguish at least three major components of functionalism: functionalist theory, terminological scheme, and method. Let us at this point discuss these aspects briefly.

Functionalist Theory

Is functionalism a social theory? Superficially, some functionalists, as well as their critics, would answer affirmatively. For example, Davis (1959) is quite explicit on this point: "Functionalism is preeminently social theory [p. 761]." Similarly, such leading critics of functionalism as R. Dahrendorf, D. Lockwood, and C. Wright Mills apparently attack it as a particular theoretical *Weltanschauung*. There is an implicit suggestion to the same effect in phrases such as: "functional theory of culture," "theory of needs," "functional theory of stratification," "theory of the social system," etc. It is the analyst's privilege not to accept such declarations at face value. I will exercise this privilege and argue that there is no functional theory.

Of course, as I stressed previously, one may use the term *theory* loosely and call any and every product of scientific research by this name. It is not an uncommon practice in sociology, presumably because of the favorable connotations the term *theory* has acquired in the discipline. There is hardly any term in sociology (with the possible exception of the term *model*) more abused. But if we hold to the meaning of theory that was specified in the preceding chapters, it may easily be shown that what professes to be a functional theory never satisfies all the criteria of an explanatory system.

Let us take a brief look at the most widely discussed of functional "theories," Davis and Moore's theory of stratification. The deficiencies of this "theory," which in fact deny its being a theory at all (at least in our sense of the term), seem to be fairly typical of the so-called "functionalist theories."

The Davis–Moore theory may be reconstructed as an explanatory system consisting of the number of explanations on several levels. On the primary level, we have the following explanation:

Explanans
1. Without a certain amount of stratification, i.e., institutionalized inequality or differentiation of persons in terms of both prestige and esteem, there will be no possibility of filling the positions of social structure with qualified and properly motivated persons.

"The main functional necessity explaining the universal presence of stratification is precisely the requirement faced by any society of placing and motivating individuals in the social structure [Davis and Moore 1945: 242]."

2. If the positions of social structure are not filled with qualified and properly motivated persons, the society cannot persist. "As a functioning mechanism society must somehow distribute its members in social positions and induce them to perform the duties of these positions [Davis and Moore 1945: 242]."

3. Societies do persist (implicit assumption).

Explanandum
Phenomenon of stratification (institutionalized inequality of differentiation of persons in terms of both prestige and esteem) is ubiquitous in human society. "Every society, no matter how simple or complex, must differentiate persons in terms of both prestige and esteem, and must therefore possess a certain amount of institutionalized inequality [Davis and Moore 1945: 243]."

On the second level, the main explaining premise is transformed into a secondary explanandum and explained further in the following way:

Explanans
1. There is a differential functional importance of positions, and relative scarcity of personnel for filling more important positions.
2. To fill functionally more important positions, more skills, talents, and consequently more training is necessary.
3. Training implies some sacrifices on the part of the person trained.
4. It is necessary for the society to motivate some people to take up the training enabling them to fill the more important positions.
5. The only way to motivate people to sacrifice something is to reward them with special perquisites associated with positions they are going to obtain as a result of sacrifice (basic motivational assumption).
6. Differential perquisites of positions imply differential prestige and esteem.

Explanandum
Without the presence of stratification the positions in the social structure could not be filled properly.

I need not pursue a substantive criticism of each proposition separately. This has been done more than extensively in the sociological literature (see Tumin 1953, Huaco 1966, Simpson 1956, Buckley 1958, and others). My point is that this is not a full-fledged theory, but at most an "explanatory sketch." To support this assertion, let me examine the Davis–Moore "theory" in light of the seven requirements of a theory made precise in the preceding chapters.

First, the primary explanandum of the theory is neither sufficiently specified, nor sufficiently justified. There is a great deal of misunderstanding as to the meaning of stratification in the explained proposition, and one may also ask what is the rigorous basis for claiming the universal presence of stratification in human societies, apart from common-sense evidence.

Second, the explanatory system is not valid. The scope of the explanandum is not matched to the scope of the explanans. The proposition in the explanandum is explicitly conceived as universal, while the propositions in the explanans are at most historical generalizations of a limited scope.

Third, some of the propositions included in the explanans are clearly not testable. For example, there seems to be no operational way of determining the degrees of functional importance of certain positions, short of some common-sense considerations; e.g., whether generals are functionally more important than soldiers, and directors than typists.

Fourth, almost all of the propositions lack sufficient empirical evidence to be considered as confirmed and not hypothetical.

Fifth, the theory is not complete. It raises more questions than it solves. Almost all of the propositions included in the secondary explanans can be subjected to further explanation, and the same is true of the second premise of the primary explanation which is left as a given.

Sixth, the criterion of consistency cannot be applied because the explanatory system is not complete (see earlier).

Seventh, the explanatory system is isolated—it is not unified with other explanatory systems.

The exercise of verifying these charges is left to the reader. I propose that similar deficiencies are found in other functionalist theories as well. Thus, one is forced to agree with Homans (1964): "The trouble with their [functional] theory was not that it was wrong, but that it was not a theory [p. 813]."

Functionalist Terminological Scheme

The critics of functionalism are especially fond of treating it as a particular terminological scheme and nothing more. Some functionalists themselves are also quite explicit in qualifying their own results as "conceptual schemes," "a generalized system of theoretical categories," "a structure of conceptual elements," or "a conceptual frame of reference." Yet they are rarely consistent, and a page or two later speak of "theory" or "theoretical system." One must be very clear as to the basic differences between these two types of scientific results.

By a terminological scheme I mean a more or less ordered set of nominally defined terms and analytical categories which serve to identify and classify certain elements within a given universe of discourse. In different terms, it is a sort of technical "dictionary" useful in speaking about a specific subject matter. Any interrelations among concepts or terms within the scheme have purely an analytic character, they result from the accepted meanings of the terms and not from any contingent properties of objective reality.

I think that large parts of the work of Parsons, Levy, Easton, Loomis, and many others fit very well within the given definition of terminological scheme. We are dealing here with immensely elaborate and internally coherent systems of categories which aim at characterizing basic aspects of human action, the social system, social structure, and social processes. These imposing constructions are, however, totally divorced from empirical reality; the predicated relationships (if any) do not describe or explain facts, but rather the implications of adopted definitions. As Moore (1967) noted: "In the case of the neo-scholastics I submit, the relationships do not derive from the objective materials examined but for the most part from the verbal symbols alone [p. 334]." The same point is made by Homans (1971):

> What the functionalists actually produced was not a theory but a new language for describing social structure, one among many possible languages; and much of the work they called theoretical consisted in showing how the words in other languages, including that of everyday life, could be translated into theirs. . . . But what makes a theory is deduction, not translation [p. 108].

Functionalist Method

Functionalism is a particular method of sociological inquiry. More and more frequently, functionalism is referred to as "a methodological orientation," "an analytic method," "an interpretative framework," or "a research strategy."

One must be very clear as to the sense in which functionalism is a method—the more so because critical evaluations of this aspect of functionalism take basically contradictory forms. On the one hand is the claim that there is no specific functional method because in its essence every sociological method (save some reductionistic approaches) is functional. This is the position taken by Davis (1959) on the myth of functional analysis. On the other hand, we encounter the claim that the functional method, at least in some of its aspects, is a specific approach to social reality, quite distinct from other approaches. (This is the position to be defended in subsequent chapters.)

By the sociological method I shall mean the totality of rules of procedure covering the whole process of sociological inquiry from the statement of the problem, through its operationalization, the gathering of relevant data, their interpretation, organization or systematization, up to the end-product consisting of an explanatory system of verified assertions about social reality. It is immediately to be seen that the set of rules comprising sociological method is not homogeneous. It seems well to distinguish at least three subsets of methodological rules dealing with distinct phases of the research process: (a) heuristic maxims suggesting the most fruitful ways of selecting important problems; (b) empirical techniques defining the specific means of data-gathering; and (c) methods of theory construction defining the ways in which data should be interpreted, organized, and systematized into meaningful explanatory wholes. All three subsets of methodological rules can be distinguished within the functional method. They are discussed in turn, and in this way we shall arrive at the final delimitation of the proper field of subsequent analysis.

Heuristic Maxims of Functionalism

The recognition of the heuristic import of functionalism is quite common. It is to be found in the works of its earliest advocates. Malinowski (1969) was quite explicit on this point: "I suggest the concept of function, with reference to certain wide, separate, institutional groups, primarily as a heuristic device [p. 170]." A similar idea was expressed by Radcliffe-Brown (1952):

> The concept of function as defined above constitutes a "working hypothesis" by which a number of problems are formulated for investiga-

tion. . . . The hypothesis does not require the dogmatic assertion that everything in the life of every community has a function. It only requires the assumption that it may have one, and that we are justified in seeking to discover it [p. 184].

In sociology the heuristic aspect of the functionalist method is also stressed very often. Discussing the differences between the causal and functional approaches, Merton pointed out the different problems implied by each of them, and different questions that could be posed meaningfully in the contexts of each. (cf. Loomis, and Loomis 1961: 614) The same observation was made by Davis (in Goode, 1951) in the introduction to Goode's monograph, *Religion Among the Primitives:* "My opinion is that the sole difference between a functionalist and a nonfunctionalist lies in the kind of questions raised [p. 13]. . . . The value of such a conceptual framework is the direction it gives to inquiry and the chance it offers to use empirical investigation for genuine scientific development [p. 17]." Similar remarks appear in philosophical evaluations of functionalism. Hempel (1959), in his discussion of the logic of functional analysis, wrote: "What is often called functionalism is best viewed not as a body of doctrine or theory advancing tremendously general principles . . . , but rather as a program for research guided by certain heuristic maxims, or working hypotheses [p. 301]."

Let us present some examples of heuristic maxims representative of the functional approach. The basic one would be, "If you want to understand a particular social phenomenon, look for its role in the wider social or cultural context." More particular ones would be: "Do not be satisfied with the motives given by actors for their actions, look for objective consequences." "Search for those objective consequences of a given action or given institution which are not recognized and intended by the actors." "Look not only for the positive consequences that a given action or institution has for the social whole in which it is included, but also for negative consequences." "Look for alternative structural components that can perform the same or similar roles in the same social or cultural context." "Look for the necessary structural arrangements in the system, lacking which it could not survive intact."

This enumeration is only illustrative and certainly not complete. But it is sufficient to indicate two general points. First, functional heuristic directives are specific; that is, they are in no way common to any and every sociological research. In this sense, the functional approach is distinct in sociology. Second, from the logical point of view, the heuristic directives are not assertions, but rather instrumental statements. They cannot be considered as true or false, but only as fruitful or not in attaining a given end (in this case, understanding social phenomena). To assess their fruitfulness is the proper task for the historian of science. Did they really fulfill their promise? Did they promote our understanding of society? Such questions can be answered only by examining "arrivals" and not "approaches" themselves.

Functionalist Empirical Techniques

There is a certain common misrepresentation of functionalism among social anthropologists. They are very often apt to equate functionalism with a particular technique of data-gathering—so-called "field research." This technique was expounded most thoroughly by Malinowski and used extensively in his empirical studies. Let us outline the basic features of "field research" as conceived by Malinowski (1922).

The basic principle requires that "Each phenomenon ought to be studied through the broadest range possible of its concrete manifestations; each studied by an exhaustive survey of detailed examples [p. 17]." This principle implies more particular research ways. There are three sources of empirical materials that can be utilized. The first is intensive participant observation directed at all aspects of social structure and culture, as well as to so-called "imponderabilia of actual life"—features of human behavior such as "the routine of a man's working day, the details of his care of the body, of the manner of taking food and preparing it [Malinowski 1922: 18]." The second source of information is the anthropological interview held in the language of the community and aimed at uncovering the state of social consciousness, or as Malinowski put it: "primitive mentality." The interview is concerned with all the comments, interpretations, ritual formulas, typical expressions, myths, etc., as they are phrased by the people themselves. The third source of materials consists of the official archives that are often to be found for postcolonial territories.

The data from these manifold sources are included in the ethnographic notebook. They are supplemented by maps, sketches, graphic representations, etc. The next step consists of arranging the data in "synoptic tables," dividing them into categories, and rearranging them according to several criteria. This is considered as a point of departure for any wider generalizations and a significant step in the "method of statistic documentation by concrete evidence."

There is certainly much more to be said about the techniques of "field research." But, and this is an important point, all this is presently to be found in every handbook of social research: It is no longer the property of a particular school or intellectual orientation. The link between functionalism and field research is a historical, but only a historical, fact. It is probably true that the complex, comprehensive data being gathered by means of this technique contributed to the creation of a particular image of society as a whole of interconnected elements. This point was made by Beattie (1964):

> To perceive causal connections between different social institutions in reallife situations it is first of all necessary to understand these institutions thoroughly; to know both how they work and what those who participate in them think about them. . . . And this kind of understanding, at least in exotic and unfamiliar contexts, was impossible until intensive field studies of working communities began to be made [p. 51].

In this sense there is perhaps a definite historical link between the field technique and the functional theory of culture. But this link does not exist any longer. The technique of field research is presently used by scholars who are not functionalists. And, on the other hand, one may be a functionalist utilizing different, more indirect techniques of data-gathering (e.g., questionnaires). The technique that developed in anthropology is now applied almost universally.

Functionalist Strategy of Theory Construction

I suggest that the importance of functionalism does not inhere in its theory, nor in its terminological scheme, but rather in its method. I also claim that within the functional method as a whole, that aspect most specific for functionalism and at the same time most significant for present-day sociology is the way of interpreting and organizing, or systematizing, sociological data into the meaningful structures of an explanatory system. I will refer to this aspect of the functional method as *functional analysis. Functional analysis* is here conceived as a particular method of theory construction, a particular way of explaining social phenomena. Here is to be found the "rational core" of the functionalist orientation and the lasting contribution of functionalism to social science.

In turn, the core of functional analysis is the conceptual model of society which informs the propositions incorporated into functionalist theory and generates the specific explanatory structures characteristic of such a theory. The reconstruction, critical appraisal, and generalization of this conceptual model will occupy our attention in the remaining chapters of this volume.

The crucial phase of this study will naturally be a reconstruction. It seems much easier to agree on a set of evaluative criteria than on the characteristics of the evaluated object, the more so with respect to an object so ambiguous and fluid as mine. I wish to emphasize four necessary traits of attempted reconstruction. First, the reconstruction will be basically descriptive; i.e., it will attempt to be as true as possible to the actual content of functional models, but it will also attempt to uncover implicit aspects of these models. Second, the reconstruction will be hypothetical. The assumptions of functional models are not always recognized by functionalists themselves. Moreover, when one tries to bring out an assumption that is not explicit, it must be considered tentative and subject to refutation. Third, the reconstruction will be selective. I shall try to explicate only those assumptions of functional models that seem to be most characteristic and distinguishing for functional analysis. But certainly any judgment as to what is most characteristic and distinguishing may always be in doubt. Fourth, the reconstruction will be eclectic or, in some special sense of the word, ahistorical. I shall pick out single ideas from the works of many functionalists, with no regard to the context in which they were formulated, the particular circumstances of their formulation, the historical period in which they were formulated, etc. I feel justified in this procedure by the fact that this is an analytic and not historical study.

As to the evaluative phase of my discussion, one remark must be made at once. The choice of evaluative criteria is based on the belief that sociology is primarily an empirical science and as such should be judged by the same criteria as any other empirical science, whether social or natural. I accept the position of methodological naturalism, claiming the unity of empirical science, at least with respect to the procedures of theory construction. This is to be sure a questionable and, in fact, often discussed assumption. It would be far beyond the scope of this volume to enter into this discussion. Therefore, I take it for granted in the present context, warning the reader that some of the evaluative conclusions are obviously informed by this assumption and simply would not make sense for anybody who would claim the basic incompatibility of the methodological standards of the natural and social sciences.

One more remark on the analytic strategy adopted in this book: As was stated earlier, each conceptual model comprises a certain number of general and particular assumptions. It is feasible to distinguish a general model, as composed of general assumptions, and a particular model, as composed of particular assumptions. Those concepts that are logically implied by a certain general model will be said to make up the *basic functionalist language*. And those concepts that are logically implied by a certain particular model will be said to make up the *specific functionalist language*. In this way a certain hierarchical order within the language of functional analysis will be created and the status of several functional concepts will be precisely determined. At the same time, a certain "horizontal" order among functional concepts will be established as well. Admittedly, each model may be more or less complex or more or less restrictive, depending on the number of assumptions it includes. Those concepts that are logically implied by the less complex (or less restrictive) models will be said to belong to the *primary functionalist language*. And those concepts that are logically implied by the more complex (or restrictive) models will be said to belong to the *secondary functionalist language*.

Obviously enough, the significance of the criticism directed against the adequacy of basic and primary concepts will be much larger than in the case of specific and secondary ones. I shall attempt to show that the neglect of this crucial difference is responsible for some faulty critiques of functional models.

Chapter 5

SYSTEMIC MODELS
IN FUNCTIONAL ANALYSIS

What is the most general image of society inherent in sociological functionalism? How is the subject matter conceived in broadest terms? Let us look at some telling remarks of representative functionalists. Radcliffe-Brown (1935) wrote: "If functionalism means anything at all, it does mean the attempt to see the social life of a people as a whole, as a functional unity [p. 634]." For Malinowski (1934, vol. III) the proper subject of anthropological study is culture. In defining culture, he wrote: "Culture is a reality sui generis and must be studied as such. . . . Culture is a well-organized unity divided into two fundamental aspects . . . [p. 623]." Later, Malinowski (1969) emphasized the same point: "Culture is an integral whole [p. 36]." "It is a system of objects, actions and attitudes in which all parts are means for a goal [p. 150]." Merton (1949) reduced "the central orientation of functionalism" to "the practice of interpreting data by establishing their consequences for the larger structures in which they are implicated . . . [pp. 46–47]." And Parsons (1964) was more explicit on this point:

> The most essential condition of successful dynamic analysis is continual and systematic reference of every problem to the state of the system as a whole . . . It is thus the functional reference of all particular conditions and processes to the state of the total system as a going concern which provides the logical equivalent of simultaneous equations in a fully developed system of analytical theory [p. 216–217].

There is obviously a common idea in the preceding remarks, despite terminological differences. Namely, the sociological subject matter—society or culture—is conceived as a particular *whole* or *system*. It is irrelevant for this analysis whether that whole is characterized in ontological terms, as a defining characteristic of a specific social form of "being" (Malinowski), or whether it is simply treated as a methodological assumption (Merton and Parsons). In both cases one encounters the image of social life as incorporated in systems. There seems to be no doubt that the most characteristic, essential feature of functionalism is the *systemic image of society* which is accepted more or less explicitly by its proponents.

More specific characteristics of society, viewed in general terms as a system, have been made precise in functionalist tradition in two different ways: per analogiam and per abstracto. Let us examine these two approaches in turn.

Organic Analogy

The first method consists of specifying some other, better-known subject matter whose essential properties and regularities are supposed to be so similar to those of the subject matter under study that it seems feasible and valid to apply the knowledge concerning the former in the analysis of the latter. When society is conceived as a system, it is almost natural to look for other examples of systems, and biological or organic systems suggest themselves immediately as the closest analogues. In effect, as Martindale (1960) observed: "The organic type of system became the primary model of functional interpretation [p. 448]."

There are several general properties of organic systems. They may be summarized, following Deutsch (1966), thus:

> An organism, according to the classic view, cannot be analyzed, at least in some of its essential parts. It cannot be taken apart and put together again without damage. Each part of a classic organism, insofar as it can be identified at all, embodies in its structure the particular function to which it has been assigned. As a rule, these parts cannot be put to any other functions without destroying the organism. The classic organism's behavior is irreversible [pp. 30–31].

These characteristics seemed to apply quite well to the primitive, closed, and isolated societies studied by social anthropologists. And

so, as Beattie (1964) remarked: "The key which opened the door
to systematic understanding of simpler, 'primitive' societies was the
organic analogy [pp. 49–50]." A structural similarity (or isomorphism)
was posited between society (or for that matter, culture) and a particular, quite specific example of a system, namely the biological organism. By force of this assumption of analogy, several conclusions
were derived concerning society or culture.

The most elaborate application of the organic analogy is to be
found in the works of A. R. Radcliffe-Brown (1952), who went so
far as to state that: "The concept of function applied to human societies is based on an analogy between social life and organic life [p.
178]." Attempting to define the concept of function, he explicitly
invoked the analogy and traced the main points of similarity between
an organism and a society. What are the main properties of the living
organism in Radcliffe-Brown's view? First of all, it is a living, integrated whole, quite different from a simple collection of unrelated
elements. There are definite links among all the elements that make
up the organic structure. Second, the living organism preserves a
certain structural continuity despite significant changes and transformations at the level of its elements. The process by which this continuity is preserved is *life*. And third, within the total process of
life, some subprocesses or phases may be distinguished. Each of them
fulfills a certain specified function.

> If we consider any recurrent part of the life-process, such as respiration,
> digestion, etc., its function is the part it plays in, the contribution
> it makes to, the life of the organism as a whole. . . . The function
> of a recurrent physiological process is thus a correspondence between
> it and the needs (i.e., the necessary conditions of existence) of the
> organism [Radcliffe-Brown 1952: 179].

And, turning to society, Radcliffe-Brown (1952) claimed that all
three properties are to be found on the social level as well. First,
human beings, the basic elements of society, are linked by a definite
network of social relations. Thus, there exists a certain social structure
which makes a society something more than a simple aggregate of
people; namely, it is a specific integrated whole. Second, continuity
of the whole is preserved, despite the constant changes and transformations at the level of the individual and, specifically, despite the
continual replacement of persons making up a given society. And
third, this continuity of structure is preserved by virtue of the specific

functions performed by the elements of social structure. "The function of any recurrent activity, such as the punishment of a crime or a funeral ceremony, is the part it plays in the social life as a whole and therefore the contribution it makes to the maintenance of the structural continuity [p. 180]."

There is great heuristic value in drawing significant analogies, but at the same time, pressing them too far may be very risky. The uncritical use of organic analogy may have dangerous consequences. The first danger is that of *reification*. It is very easy to slip from the assertion that society *may be compared* to an organism, which has mainly methodological import and is provisionally accepted as a guide for further inquiry, to the stronger, ontological claim that society *is* an organism. This is stressed by Beattie (1964), who cautioned: "We must not allow this methodological resemblance to lead us to suppose that societies are something like organisms; they are not, and to suppose that they are may lead to serious error [p. 56]."

But this is not the only danger. The more subtle one inherent in the methodological use of analogy consists of passing over differences and *dissimilarities* and stressing only points of convergence between two disparate cases of systems. In an extreme case this may lead to the attribution to the subject matter under study, not only of the general, essential properties and relations characteristic of the analogue, but also of a superfluous mass of particular, insignificant features. An analogy is always valid only in certain respects—it is by no means complete identity. Hence, it is of fundamental importance to distinguish carefully between properties or relations which constitute the *basis of analogy* between discussed subjects, and properties or relations which constitute the *basis of disanalogy* between them. Only with respect to the first set of properties or relations is the transfer of knowledge from the analogue (which is supposedly better understood) to the proper object of study logically and methodologically valid.

Let us trace the basic points of disanalogy existing between the biological organism and human society. Three groups of differences may be identified referring to: (*a*) the characteristics of the particular elements; (*b*) the characteristics of relations among the elements, or the structure of the system; and (*c*) the characteristics of the transformation of the system in time, or the dynamic process.

First, it is obvious that all the *properties of elements* are fundamentally different in the case of an organism as opposed to society. There is no conceivable similarity between, say, organic cells as the ultimate elements of an organism, and people as the ultimate elements of society. There is also no similarity between, for instance, respiration as an elementary process in an organism, and economic production as an elementary process in society. What they do have in common is that they are parts of some wider wholes or wider processes. But this similarity is vacuous and tautological; it carries no informational value. In such a wide sense all things are alike, for there is always a conceivable whole to which they belong.

Second, there are at least three points on which organic *structure* differs fundamentally from social structure. First, the integration of elements within an organic structure is extremely strong; it is impossible to conceive of an element existing outside the whole. It is only in the stories of Poe that one shakes hands long since severed from bodies. But societal integration is never so perfect. Individuals and groups are able to cut off all links with the whole and still survive. Outcasts, deviants, marginal people, as well as revolutionaries of all brands, are suitable examples. Second, the specialization of elements and processes is obviously much more pronounced in the case of an organism than in society. It is impossible to think with one's legs and to walk with one's brain. On the other hand, the philosopher may once in a while cut firewood, and the woodcutter write philosophical treatises. And finally, there is the profound difference having to do with the lack of a common controlling "sensorium" in the case of society, as opposed to its clear presence in the case of an organism. Many hypostases, and reifications such as the "collective soul," the "will of the nation," etc., have their intellectual source in the rejection of this significant difference.

Third, the course of *dynamic changes* takes quite different forms in an organism as opposed to society. Two points of disanalogy seem most important in this respect. The particular organism may undergo only internal changes (growth, metabolism, adaptation, compensation, aging, etc., are easy examples of processes taking place within the same, basically unchanging structure). But in the realm of society, changes may obviously be of different forms; they may consist of more or less radical transformations of the social structure itself. Apart from intrasystemic change, which may be defined in Cancian's (1960) terms as a "change that does not alter the system's basic structure [p. 823]," society may undergo extrasystemic change: "any change that alters the system's basic structure [Cancian 1960; 823]." The same point is made by Radcliffe-Brown (1952): "An animal organism does not, in the course of its life, change its structural type. A pig does not become a hippopotamus. . . . On the other hand a society in the course of its history can and does change its structural type without any break of continuity [p. 181]." Uncritical use of the organic analogy has done most harm precisely at this point. The static bias of some schools of contemporary functionalism may be traced to this misapplication.

A correlative point of disanalogy has to do with the course of organic, as opposed to social, changes. The first have a cyclical character, run according to predetermined phases of growth, maturity, decay, death, and have easily specified starting points as well as terminal points. The second have, in certain important respects, a directive, irreversible character, lacking any definite beginning, as well as any conceivable end. One may call it development, progress, or evolution. But there is certainly no similar phenomenon in the case of a single organism (on the ontogenetic level). Dismissal of this fundamental difference has led directly to the ahistoric bias of some schools of contemporary functionalism.

In conclusion, one must agree with Anderson and Moore (1966) that the use of organic analogy for explaining social phenomena has just about the same degree of cogency as "if the child asked us how a bird flies, and if we then pointed to a flying airplane and said: Look, that's how it's done [p. 88]."

System as Generalized Notion

A growing awareness of the hazards presented by the organic analogy has led to the abandonment of this method of specification of systemic notions and to its replacement by a new approach. To grasp the basic idea of this new method of defining a system, let us look again at the points of similarity and disparity between organisms and societies. A certain regularity may then be observed; the points of similarity refer to the most abstract, so to say, generic properties, while the points of difference refer to the most particular properties. For example, whereas the general feature of possessing some kind of structure, i.e., a set of interconnections between elements, is characteristic of both entities, the particular type of internal integration varies in each case. The same is true of the general feature of compensatory capabilities within some range of external disturbances versus the particular "mechanism" by means of which the compensation is carried on in each of the cases. There are certainly many more similar examples.

The lesson in all this is simple: Both an organism and a society are generically, but only generically, similar; they are two cases of the same type. The generic features that constitute the basis of analogy, define the type and the particular features that constitute the basis of disanalogy, define diverse, individual cases within the type. Therefore, instead of interpreting society in terms of some specific parallel case of the same type (e.g., an organism), it seems much more promising to abstract the properties of the type itself and interpret society in these general terms. When this lesson is learned, the basic dimensions of every conceivable system are specified, and some of them are posited as the characteristic, defining features of the social system. This approach avoids the danger of applying specific, and as such irrelevant, properties of an analogue to the proper object under study. As Gouldner (1959) put it: "The need to distinguish between the concrete case, namely the organism, and the thing it was a case of, namely a system, became increasingly evident to functional theorists [p. 242]."

Thus we come to the second method of defining the social system; no longer per analogiam, but rather per abstracto. This method is characteristic of modern functionalism. Basically it consists of the generalization and relativization of the concept of a system.

Generalization proceeds by means of isolating those fundamental structural properties which may characterize any system, and then selecting a particular set of those fundamental properties which lend themselves to characterizing social reality. As Gouldner (1959) described it: "A second route . . . is to make explicit the most generalized dimensions in terms of which systems, formally construed, may vary and then to stipulate the conjunction of formal system dimensions which are to be applied to social behavior [p. 242]." This procedure escapes the danger of being "a focus on characteristics which were peculiar to the organism but not inherent in a generalized notion of a system [Gouldner 1959: 241]."

Relativization is the double expansion of the domain to which the notion of a system is applied. The use of the organic analogy was usually restricted to global societies, defined in spatiotemporal terms, and seen as comprised of individual human beings or, at most, of collectivities. It was Andaman society that constituted a social organism for Radcliffe-Brown. In present-day functionalism, both the system itself and its components are conceived in a less restrictive way. One trend of relativization may be considered as realistic, in the philosophical sense of the term. The system is construed as a real whole, existing "out there," but it is exemplified not only by global societies, but also by less inclusive social wholes such as social groups, communities, etc. This trend brought about the schism between two branches of contemporary functionalism: macrofunctionalism, applying a systemic framework, in the old tradition, to global societies, and microfunctionalism, for which the system of reference is a human group—especially a "small group" (cf. Martindale 1960). The second trend of relativization, and a much more important one, represents some assumptions of nominalistic (or even conventionalistic) philosophy. It construes a system as a useful tool for identifying certain important complexes or networks of social relations—economy, polity, culture, society, and social personality. Here a system becomes more an analytical instrument than a representation of some ontological entity.

The generalized and relativized concept of system may be specified on two distinct levels of abstraction: the analytic level and the concrete level. On the *analytic level* the social system is conceived in terms of variables, relations, roles, statuses, and the like. On the *concrete level* the social system is conceived in terms of people, their interactions, collectivities, groups, classes, etc. Whereas on the concrete level all concepts defining the social system have immediate empirical referents, on the analytic level they have the logical status of abstract constructs with no immediate empirical reference. This distinction is tantamount to one made by Lockwood (1964) between social integration and system integration: "Whereas the problem of social integration focuses attention upon the orderly or conflictual relationships between the actors, the problem of system integration focuses on the orderly or conflictual relationships between the parts of a social system [p. 245]." A similar distinction has been introduced in various contexts by other authors (cf. Levy 1952: 88–89; Bredemeier and Stephenson 1962: 35). Much confusion has resulted from the neglect of fundamental differences between the analytic level and the concrete level in the study of social systems.

There seems to be a clear dominance of the analytic perspective in definitions of social systems. And this applies not only to the functionalism of Merton, Parsons, Levy, and others, but also to the functionalism of Malinowski and Radcliffe-Brown. For the founders of functionalism the concept of culture represents the similar analytic aspects of society which are covered by the notion of a social system in more modern usage. On the nature of culture, Malinowski (1969) wrote:

> Culture is an integral composed of partly autonomous, partly coordinated institutions. It is integrated on a series of principles such as the community of blood through procreation; the contiguity in space related to cooperation; the specialization of activities; and last but not least the use of power in political organization [p. 40].

Thus, the basic elements of culture (read, society) are clearly not individual people, nor objects, but social relations. It is certainly true that Malinowski was rarely consistent in his writings and he sometimes switched to a concrete perspective. But it is well to point out that the analytic approach was not alien to his image of culture.

The focus on an analytic level is much more obvious in the works of sociological adherents to functionalism. In the common exposition of their approach, the authors of *Toward A General Theory of Action* gave this definition: "The social system is composed of relationships of individual actors and only of such relationships. . . . For most analytic purposes, the most significant unit of social structure is not the person but the role [Parsons and Shils 1951: 23]." Parsons (1951) offered quite a similar characterization of a social system: "It is the structure of the relations between the actors as involved in the interactive process which is essentially the structure of the social system. The system is a network of such relationships [p. 25]." And a similar point was made by Levy (1952): "It is important to keep in mind that the system of action in operation is the society as the term is used here. A society in this sense is not a group [p. 122]."

The *generalized, relative*, and *analytic* notion of a system is the central category of functionalist thinking, and the most significant achievement of the school. Gouldner (1959) was correct in considering it "an intellectual fundament of functional theory in sociology [p. 241]." I would add only that this is a fundament on which much can be built in the future. To save this fundament is precisely the purpose of this book.

Functional Analysis and Systems Approach

The recognition that the core of functionalism is the systemic model of society is crucial for the reconstruction and appraisal of functional analysis. Namely, the adoption of a systemic frame of reference places functional analysis in the mainstream of some very important tendencies of contemporary science. Functional analysis may be regarded as a branch of what is widely known as "systems approach," "systemic analysis," or "general systems theory."

The *systemic approach* gives evidence of being a very useful method of interpreting a wide array of problems in various disciplines of science, not only, and even not preeminently, in the social sciences. Some authors consider it a basic reorientation of scientific thinking in general, the redefinition of the paradigm, the retreat from the atomistic and mechanistic approach of the nineteenth century toward a holistic image of reality. According to one of the advocates of the systemic approach, L. Von Bertalanffy (1968):

> We may state as characteristic of modern science that the scheme of isolable units acting in one-way causality has proved to be insufficient. Hence, the appearance in all fields of science of notions like wholeness, holistic, organismic, Gestalt, etc., which all signify that in the last resort we must think in terms of elements in mutual interaction [p. 45].

This view is shared by Ackoff (1959): "In the last two decades we have witnessed the emergence of the system as a key concept in scientific research [p. 17]." And Sadovsky and Yudin (1967) predicted: "the gradual inclusion of all science into a systemic–structural framework."

I consider functionalism in sociology as a particular implementation of the systemic approach, and functional analysis as a specific form of systemic analysis. In order to appraise the sense in which it is particular and specific, one must be very precise as to the character of systemic conceptual models assumed by functionalists. There is an array of systemic models of society underlying functionalist thinking. Some of them are more complex, comprising a larger number of general assumptions, and some are less complex, comprising a smaller number of general assumptions. Each general assumption generates some particular dimensions of possible structural variability within the model, and the concrete values of variables along each of these dimensions must also be specified. Thus, some models are less restrictive, allowing for more freedom of decision in determining structural properties of the model, and some are more restrictive, implying more necessary decisions as to the particular structural features of the model.

I propose to distinguish *five types of systemic–functional models* in order of growing complexity and restrictiveness:

1. The model of a simple system
2. The model of a teleological system
3. The model of a functional system
4. The model of a purposeful system
5. The model of a multiple system

This distinction affords a convenient basis for constructing a typology of functional analysis. I agree with Mulkay (1971) that "there are many varieties of functional analysis [p. 3]." Each should be discussed and judged separately, for each is applicable in different contexts, and each faces different challenges. I propose to distinguish *five types of functional analysis* taking into account the type of systemic–functional model adopted in each case:

1. The simple functional analysis
2. The directive functional analysis
3. The functional–requisite analysis
4. The functional–motivational analysis
5. The functional–subsystemic analysis

All these types of systemic–functional models, and all the forms of functional analysis conceived as a specific method of theory construction, are reconstructed and appraised in the next five chapters.

Chapter 6

SIMPLE
FUNCTIONAL ANALYSIS

The Model of a Simple System

The model of a simple system consists of that minimum set of assumptions that seems to be necessarily presupposed by any and every functional analysis. These assumptions are not exclusive; most functionalists do not restrict themselves to accepting them only, but rather make some additional assumptions. We shall discuss the more complex and restrictive functional models in later chapters. The model that concerns us at present is fundamental in the sense that its assumptions are adopted of logical necessity by any functional analysis, though they usually are supplemented by some additional ones.

The model of a simple system is made up of four general assumptions. The first defines the general nature of society as a complex set of elements. The second characterizes that complex of elements as a specific whole. The third defines the character of internal integration typical for that whole. The fourth defines the external relationships binding the whole with the other fragments of the world.

The assumption of plurality claims that society consists of set of elements (defined either in realistic terms as concrete objects, structures, etc., or in nominalistic terms as variables, states, etc.). This assumption is fairly evident and requires little discussion. It may be found explicitly in some of the Malinowski's (1969) definitions of culture: "It consists of implements and consumer goods, of constitutional charters for the various social groupings, of human ideas and crafts, beliefs, and customs [p. 36]." The plurality of elements (in this case social relations) is also considered as a defining feature of a social system by Parsons and Shils (1951): "Any system of interactive relationships of a plurality of individual actors is a social system [p. 26]"; as well as by Parsons (1951): "A social system consists in a plurality of individual actors interacting with each other in a situation [p. 5]."

The assumption of wholeness claims that society is a specific whole having particular properties of its own that are irreducible to the properties of the elements (emergent features). The source of these particular, global properties is sought in the interrelations of single elements within the whole. The notion of a whole is ambiguous: It is certainly a relational concept that may be understood only in contradistinction to a correlative concept of an element or part. There are several meanings of the "part–whole" relation. The meaning that seems most significant for the functionalistic interpretation of the whole is specified by Nagel (1963) thus: "A whole is a set of interrelated parts, where by a part we mean either separate objects, or their attributes or states, or the processes they go through, or smaller nets of structural relationships [p. 138]." The concept of wholeness so conceived enters as a defining criterion into the most general definitions of a system. For example, Hall and Fagen (1956) concluded their discussion of the notion of a system with the following definition: "A system is a set of objects together with relationships between the objects and between their attributes [p. 18]."

It is easily seen that the assumption of wholeness says only that there are some elements and that these elements do not constitute the diffuse aggregate or, to use Sorokin's term, "congery," but rather they are bound together by certain interrelations. The assumption does not specify what the elements are nor what type of interrelations binds them together. This issue is taken up by the next assumption.

The assumption of integration claims that the relations between the elements of the whole are very close, and that this type of close relationship is characteristic for all the elements. Each part of a society is conceived to be directly, or at least indirectly, interlinked with all other parts in a regular, nonrandom manner. An element which is not influenced by others in some ways, and which does not influence others in some ways, is by definition excluded from the system. Such an internally integrated system is sometimes referred to as a *functional whole* in contradistinction to an *additive whole,* and is seen as characterized by "the connection between its component parts so close and organic, that to change one necessarily involves changing the others and often the whole system [Afanasyev 1963: 32]." A very similar idea is put forward by Sorokin (1967):

> Any cultural synthesis is to be regarded as functional, when, on the one hand, the elimination of one of its important elements perceptibly influences the rest of the synthesis in its functions (and usually in its structure) and when, on the other hand, the separate element, being transposed to a quite different combination, either cannot exist in it or has to undergo a profound modification to become a part of it. Such is the symptomatic barometer of internal integration . . . [p. 101].

The assumption of boundary claims that the intensity of interrelations between the elements of the system is significantly stronger than the intensity of interrelations between the objects or variables not being considered as elements (and thus, a boundary between the system and its environment can be precisely delineated.) It entails the rejection of the idea of isolation or independence of society from other fragments of the empirical world. And, consequently, it allows for a classification of any element from the point of view of a given system into intrasystemic and extrasystemic categories.

Among the extrasystemic elements are those which are neutral, or indifferent, for the system in the sense that they neither influence the intrasystemic elements, nor are influenced by them in any significant respect. On the other hand, one may distinguish those elements which influence the system and are influenced by the system in a significant respect. These and only these elements constitute the *environment* of the system. Hall and Fagen (1956) defined this notion in similar terms: "For a given system, the environment is the set of all objects a change in whose attributes affects the system, and also those objects whose attributes are changed by the behavior of the system [p. 20]."

One further distinction may be introduced. Namely, in the case of unilateral influence, flowing from the environment to the system, one may speak of the *parameters* of the system, the factors that from the systems' point of view are given.

To sum up, the assumption of a boundary may be construed as

a simple assertion that every system has some significant environment with which it interacts. In the words of Afanasyev (1968):

> There is no whole . . . existing for itself, in isolation. Each whole has a particular relationship with the external environment. . . . The given whole is characterized not only by the specific composition of its elements and specific structure, but by the form of its interrelationship with the environment [p. 54].

It is obvious that a system's dependence on the environment may be more or less pronounced, and so this property of the system, like the previous ones, must be also constructed in relative, rather than absolute, terms.

The four assumptions listed in this section make up the definition of a simple system. The research implications consequent upon adoption of this conceptual model are twofold. First, the focus of attention is directed toward particular elements and their intrasystemic relationships, to the neglect of the analysis of the system itself, as a going concern. Second, the focus of attention is directed toward relationships of the "part–part" type, to the neglect of relationships of the "part–whole" type. The type of functional analysis characterized by the adoption of the simple-system model (whether explicit or implicit) and, consequently, by the research priorities mentioned earlier, will be termed *simple functional analysis*.

What is the essence of this type of functional analysis? Simplifying the matter a little bit, it may be reconstructed in the following way: Within the framework of a society or culture conceived as a whole, some particular elements are singled out (institutions, modes of social action, norms, values, social relationships, etc.), and their interrelationships are thoroughly examined. The selected single element is the focus of attention, and analysis consists of specifying the various effects produced by this element for other elements of the same system. The effects of the presence (or activity) of a given element on the other elements of the same system are considered as functions of that element. The explicit definition of function in similar terms is formulated by Kaberry (1957): "The function of a certain institution or custom is its effect on the other institutions or customs [p. 80]." Nagel (1961) included this meaning in his discussion of several concepts implied by the term *function:* "This term is widely applied for signifying the relation of dependence or interdependence between two or more variable factors [p. 523]."

This meaning of function is not the only one encountered within sociological functionalism. To distinguish various meanings of function, I shall apply numerical subscripts. And thus, to rephrase and make more precise our first definition of function, one may say:

The FUNCTION$_1$ of an element E_1 in the system S is $R(E_2)$ where
1. E_1 contributes to the attainment or maintenance of the state R of E_2.
2. R is some selected elementary state of E_2 among the states included in the empirical range of possible variability of E_2.
3. E_1 and E_2 are the elements of the same system S.

It seems to me that the bulk of empirical "field studies" carried out by the earliest functionalists, as well as by their successors in anthropology, may be reconstructed as simple functional analyses, in the sense specified here. Let us consider as our first example some of the works of Malinowski. He stated as the primary purpose of empirical field research the discovery of hidden, unexpected interrelations between various elements and spheres of social life. As Richards (1957) aptly observed, for Malinowski:

> The explanation of anthropological facts lies not only in the part they play within an integral system of culture, but also in the manner in which they are related to each other within the system, and in which the system is related to the physical surroundings [p. 18]. . . . It gave rise to a continuous study of the relationships between the different aspects and institutions of a tribal society [p. 20].

And as Malinowski (1934) himself was led to remark: "The nature of culture may be reduced to the relationships between cultural elements [p. 625]." In *Argonauts of the Western Pacific,* Malinowski traced the repercussions of a specific intertribal economic exchange (the "Kula ring") in all domains of social life; for example, in the forms of family life, magical beliefs, myths, organization and technology of production, religious rituals, primitive world view, and the like. In *Coral Gardens and Their Magic,* the institution of primitive gardening is analyzed from the vantage point of its consequences for several spheres of culture and social structure; e.g., kinship, political power, property and inheritance rules, magic and religious beliefs, language, etc. Martindale (1960) observed well that "Malinowski identifies functionalism with the study of interrelations [p. 457]."

A more recent example of simple functional analysis may be found in the classic work of W. I. Goode (1951) in which he carried out an extensive study of religious institutions in selected primitive societies, focusing on the links between religious phenomena and other spheres of social life—the economic, political, familiar, etc.

One wonders if criticisms that functional analysis is equivalent to sociological analysis as such are not true with respect to simple functional analysis. As Martindale (1960) noted: "When functionalism is taken to mean interrelation, it has to be dismissed as a special theory. If there were no more to functionalism than this, every school of sociological thought would have to be described as functionalistic [p. 654]." However, there is a great deal more to functionalism than this, and within the general framework of a simple-system model, there is a wide range of possible differences concerning the particular structural assumptions. Here certain specific theoretical biases distinguishing traditional functionalism from other sociological orientations should become clear.

I shall attempt to reconstruct four dimensions of variability permitted by the general model of a simple system. Particular assumptions of this model will be conceived as extreme, or polar, types, signifying the opposite, extreme values along these dimensions.

Reciprocity versus Exploitation

The general assumptions of the simple-system model imply that the elements of the system are mutually interrelated. But the type of interrelation is left unspecified. Within the framework set by the general assumptions, several solutions of this problem may be posited. Two opposite, extreme solutions will be discussed. The first, the assumption of functional reciprocity, claims that the relationships among the elements of the system are fully symmetrical and all the exchanges between them equivalent. The second, the assumption of exploitation, claims that the relationships among the elements of the system are not symmetrical, and all exchanges between them always bring benefit to one and loss to the other.

The *assumption of reciprocity* implies an image of society in which all transfers of values between the elements (individuals, groups, institutions, etc.) are equitable; they involve either identical, homeomorphic values or diverse, heteromorphic values that have nevertheless the same relative position on some common socially accepted scale. Within this image, reciprocity is considered as the normal, prevailing state of society, and even more, as a precondition of society's continuance. All possible deviations from the pattern of reciprocity are accompanied by certain compensatory social arrangements tending to restore reciprocity in the long run. Without a certain degree of reciprocity, society would simply disintegrate. These points were stressed by Gouldner (1959):

> (1) Any one structure is more likely to persist if it is engaged in reciprocally functional interchanges with some others; (1.1) the less reciprocal the functional interchange between structures, the less likely is either structure, or the patterned relation between them, to persist, (1.2) unless compensatory mechanisms are present [p. 249].

He cites some examples of compensatory mechanisms tending to create an initial social imbalance. They include several social norms sanctioning unequivalent exchanges, but most of all, they center on the factor of power: "Power arrangements may serve to compel continuances of services for which there is little functional reciprocity [Gouldner 1959: 249–250]."

The assumption of reciprocity entails particular research priorities. Interest is focused on symmetrical, equivalent relationships, and only in the case of an obvious asymmetry is it turned to compensatory arrangements, supposedly contrived to deal with the lack of reciprocity.

This approach seems dominant in functionalist thinking. Gouldner (1960) was undoubtedly correct that: "Some concept of reciprocity has been smuggled into the basic . . . postulates of functional analysis [p. 163]." A most explicit espousal of the assumption of reciprocity is found in the works of Malinowski. In *Crime and Customs in Savage Society*, Malinowski (1926) considered the principle of reciprocity as the main mechanism explaining "why the people keep their obligations." It is "a social mechanism of binding force, based on the mutual services, . . . an integral result of the immanent symmetry of all the social transactions, the symmetry of reciprocity of services lacking which no primitive society could exist [p. 25]." He suggests that this rule is general to all primitive societies: "Symmetry of structure will be found in every savage society, as the indispensable basis of reciprocal obligations [*Ibid.*]." It pervades all spheres of primitive life, and not only economic exchanges. The long direct or indirect chains of reciprocal services are the main factor explaining the order, uniformity, and cohesion of primitive societies (Malinowski 1926: 46).

The polar opposite to the assumption of reciprocity is that of *exploitation*. The image of society implied by this alternative assumption is radically different. All transfers of values between elements (individuals, groups, institutions, etc.) are seen as not equitable: They involve different values, both in the homeomorphic and heteromorphic sense. Within this image, exploitation is considered the normal state of society, and a precondition for society's constant change.

The assumption of exploitation points to research priorities distinct from those of the reciprocity assumption. Interest is focused on asymmetrical, nonequivalent relationships. In cases of clear-cut symmetry, however, particular social mechanisms are sought which may be held responsible for counteracting, or concealing, inherent exploitation.

I am far from arguing that such an approach is typically functionalist: It certainly is not. Yet I wish to emphasize most forcefully that it is not precluded by the general framework of a simple-system model. The bias of functionalism toward reciprocal relations has nothing to do with the inherent properties of the systemic–functional frame of reference. Within the same frame of reference, the bias may be eliminated or perhaps replaced by another, for example, the assumption of exploitation.

Consensus versus Conflict

The second structural dimension of the simple-system model that leaves open the possibility of alternative, particular conceptualizations also concerns the types of relationships among elements. But this time a somewhat different aspect of these relationships is in question. Two polar assumptions may thus be distinguished. The assumption of consensus claims that the relationships between the elements of the system are congenial and harmonious, and the activity of each element may be reconciled with the activities of all others. The assumption of conflict claims that such relationships are basically antagonistic and inharmonious, and the activities of the elements are mutually incompatible and divergent.

The first assumption entails an image of society in which all elements are in perfect agreement. The ends they pursue do not contra-

dict each other, the means they adopt do not hinder each other.
There is no point at which lines of activities cross or collide. This
ideal order is seen as the normal, prevailing state of society, as a
precondition of the society's existence. Any disturbance in this picture
must be explained by extrasystemic circumstances.

The *assumption of consensus* has unique research consequences.
It requires focusing the analysis on patterned, ordered, and harmonious relationships to the exclusion of conflictual, antagonistic ones.
The latter are explained, or perhaps explained away, by the residual
category of deviance.

The assumption of consensus seems fairly typical of the functionalist
perspective. It is most explicit in the works of Parsons and his followers. As Dahrendorf (1968) commented: "According to Parsons
society is possible by virtue of some assumed general agreement on
a set of values that define the boundaries and coordinates of the
social order and of individual identity in social groups [p. 139]."
The same point is stressed by Lockwood (1964), who discussed criti-
cally "the emphatic role attributed [by Parsons] to common value
elements in the integration of social action [p. 254]." Full internalization of the ruling values by members of the society—resulting from
the process of socialization—leaves no room for dissidence and conflict. All disturbances in the peaceful, ordered world are explained
by reference to the category of deviance. But, as Dahrendorf (1968)
observed quite correctly: "Deviance occurs for sociologically—and
that means structurally—unknown and unknowable reasons. It is the
baccilus that befalls the system from the dark depth of the individual
psyche or the nebulous reaches of the outside world [p. 116]." As
a pathological phenomenon, deviance is dealt with by certain compensatory mechanisms covered by the label *social control,* which restore,
almost automatically, the disturbed consensus.

But staying within the functionalist framework, i.e., without aban-
doning its general assumptions, one may as well adopt the opposite
assumption and plead with Dahrendorf (1968) that "whenever there
is social life there is conflict" and that "not the presence but the
absence of conflict is surprising and abnormal [p. 127]." The *assumption of conflict* invokes an image of society in which there is a scarcity
of goal-satisfying values, as well as the means to reach them. The
attainment of particular goals by an element (individual, group, institution, etc.) precludes, or at least hinders, the chances of achievement
on the part of other elements. And besides, the lines of goal-seeking
activity of various elements cross at several points—the means applied

by one being incompatible with the means applied by the other. This general picture is to be encountered in various spheres of social life. As Van den Berghe (1963) put it: "Numerous societies . . . integrate widely different cultures possessing quite different value systems. Even in culturally homogeneous societies, various social groups such as classes hold antithetical political and economic values [p. 296]." From here it is only one step toward the "conflict model of society," the basic tenets of which are summarized thus by Dahrendorf (1968): "Societies and social organizations are held together not by consensus but by constraint, not by universal agreement but by the coercion of some by others. . . . Characteristic values are ruling rather than common, enforced rather than accepted [p. 127]."

The assumption of conflict calls for research priorities opposite to those of the consensus assumption. The focus of interest is upon all situations and circumstances in which elements stand in antagonistic relations to each other. Because empirical facts indicate that social relationships are sometimes harmonious, the search for particular mechanisms preventing the outbreak of conflict is deemed necessary. In Dahrendorf's (1968) view: "Conflict can be temporarily supressed, regulated, channeled, and controlled, but neither a philosopher-king nor a modern dictator can abolish it once and for all [p. 127]."

The assumption of conflict is certainly not typical of functionalism. In fact, it was proposed as a viable alternative to the functionalist perspective. But it seems to me that the inclusion of this assumption is quite compatible with the simple-system model. Once again, I claim that the bias of functionalism in favor of consensual relations has nothing to do with the inherent properties of the systemic–functional frame of reference. The same frame of reference allows equally well a bias in favor of the conflict assumption. And it also allows for a middle position. It is interesting to note that virtually the same conclusion was recently reached by Parsons: "My view has been that order and conflict are two kinds of phenomena that should be explained as obverse possibilities in terms of the same theoretical scheme [in Turk and Simpson 1971: 385]."

Dependence versus Autonomy

So far I have been focusing on the possible relationships between pairs of elements belonging to a system. The third structural dimension worth distinguishing within the simple-system model refers to the relationship of each element to the system as a whole; that is, to the totality of all the remaining elements and, vice versa, the relationship of the system as a whole to each of its elements. Some interrelation between an element and a system is of course presupposed by the very definition of a system. Nevertheless, two extreme kinds of interrelation are possible. The assumption of dependence claims that each element is interrelated with all the others and cannot exist outside the system. The assumption of autonomy claims that elements have various degrees of independence, being linked with the system only in certain restricted ways.

The *assumption of dependence* seems almost universally accepted by functionalists, both in social anthropology and in sociology. This is in part due to the communities in which anthropological field studies have been conducted: Primitive society may be viewed as a well-knit whole in which every element is fully dependent on every other. Thus, such societies would strongly satisfy the assumption of close internal integration or dependence. The existence and regular functioning of the system is directly dependent on the proper activities of the elements, and the existence of the element is totally dependent on the system, outside of which it could not possibly survive. This particular bias born within anthropological functionalism was passed on to sociologists, and especially the followers of Talcott Parsons. Heavy stress is here placed on the binding, integrating mechanisms keeping all the elements of society together. As Parsons and Shils (1951) put it: "The most general and fundamental property of a system is the interdependence of parts and variables [p. 107]." When this property is treated as absolute and constant, rather than relative and variable, the "overintegrated view of society" is the direct result (cf. Wrong 1961: 184, 190).

But remaining within the framework of a simple-system model, one may also espouse the assumption of *autonomy,* the crux of which is the recognition that "to speak of systems as characterized by an interdependence of parts and their equilibrium tends to obscure the fact that these are the things which can vary in degree [Gouldner 1959: 254]." It is necessary to regard both dependence and autonomy as problematic and to determine their actual values by empirical research, rather than by a priori postulation. This is forcefully argued by Gouldner (1959):

> . . . there are varying degrees of interdependence which may be postulated to exist among the parts of a system. At one extreme, each

element may be involved in a mutual interchange with all others; at the opposite extreme, each element may be involved in mutal interchanges with only one other. The former may be regarded as defining maximal interdependence and systemness, the latter as defining minimal interdependence or systemness [p. 245].

In the second case one may speak of a relative functional autonomy of parts. Looking from the point of view of the system, autonomy means that the system may operate regularly and persist even though some of its elements are removed. And, from the point of view of the element, it means that it is, to a significant extent, self-sufficient; it might satisfy some of its needs outside the system and, in extreme cases, can adapt itself to separation from the system. "Operationally speaking, we might say that the functional autonomy of a system part is the probability that it can survive separation from the system [*Ibid.*]."

The recognition that both assumptions, that of dependence and that of autonomy, are equally valid within the framework of systemic–functional models seems extremely important from a methodological point of view. It renders the systemic approach a more flexible means of analysis concerned with various forms of social reality, instead of restricting it to the fully integrated, totally interdependent, and cohesive societies of the past.

Isolation versus Structural Context

The last structural dimension of the simple-system model refers to the relationships of the system as a whole to its environment. Some relationship of this kind is embedded in the notion of a system as such. But the type of relationship is not determined by the general assumptions of the model. In this respect, two opposite assumptions are possible on the particular level. The *assumption of isolation* claims that the functioning of the system, and the course of intrasystemic processes, is not influenced to a significant extent by the environment, but is mainly determined by the properties inherent in the system. The *assumption of structural context* claims that the system's environment exerts an important, modifying, and determining influence on the course of intrasystemic events and processes.

The first assumption is traditionally accepted by functionalists in anthropology. The primitive societies they have been studying seem to lack a historical past, and they have not had significant contact with the wider world. They are isolated in time, as well as in space. This calls for the approach in which all social elements and processes are studied *in situ*. This particular bias, which Poggi (1965) has called an "intra-unit approach" is found to a certain degree in later sociological functionalism. The social system is examined primarily from the point of view of its internal constitution and internal functioning, with no regard for the wider context in which the system is placed. The regularities ascribed to the system are usually considered universal and valid, irrespective of the system's environment.

But in some functionalist writings, at least, the opposite assumption may be found. The recognition that the same element of the system may perform quite different functions, depending on the wider setting in which the system is situated, is becoming more and more accepted by contemporary functionalists. Discussing the functions of religion in society, Firth (1956) remarked: "The hypothesis that religion is an integrating force is more closely applicable to the simpler than to the more complex societies. With social and economic differentiation religion often becomes a banner for sectionalism [p. 242]." As another outstanding example of empirical research in which the assumption of structural context receives explicit recognition, one may quote the analysis of Geertz (1957), who attempted to account for the puzzling fact of a breakdown in the mourning ritual. A ritual commonly believed to serve positive social and psychological functions (providing for group integration and emotional stability in the face of stress-producing situations), appeared to have exactly the opposite effects in the contemporary Javanese society studied by Geertz, bringing about prolonged conflicts, antagonisms, hostilities, and even the destruction of group bonds. He saw the answer in the radical changes in the social, economic, and ideological structure of Javanese society in this century, which profoundly altered the whole structural context. Javanese communities were transformed from the socially cohesive, ideologically homogeneous, and economically autonomous units of Gemeinschaft type, to the modern Gesselschaft type society:

> In all but the most isolated parts of Java, both the simple territorial basis of village social integration and the syncretic basis of its cultural homogeneity have been progressively undermined over the past fifty years. Population growth, urbanization, monatization, and the like, have combined to weaken the traditional ties of peasant social structure; and the winds of doctrine which have accompanied the appearance

of these structural changes have disturbed the simple uniformity of religious belief and practice characteristic of an earlier period [Geertz 1957: 237].

In the changed structural context, the functions of several social institutions changed accordingly.

Certainly, there are specific objects and specific problems that can be fruitfully approached by the assumption of isolation. There are situations in which extrasystemic influences may be neglected for analytic purposes, without greatly distorting the picture. On the other hand, there are specific objects and specific problems that can be comprehended only in light of the assumption of context. Hence, in the last resort, the concrete problem must be decisive in this respect. But it is well to be aware that both approaches are equally compatible with the systemic–functional frame of reference.

The Conceptual Framework of Simple Functional Analysis

To recapitulate the conclusions of my argument: There are four general assumptions and four pairs of alternative particular assumptions that constitute the model of a simple system. These assumptions are logically presupposed by a simple functional analysis, the first type of functional analysis that has been distinguished. Some concepts applied in simple functional analysis are intrinsically linked with general assumptions; they make sense only if general assumptions are accepted. I call them the basic concepts. And some concepts are intrinsically linked with particular assumptions; they make sense only if particular assumptions are accepted. I call them specific concepts.

The language of simple functional analysis contains three basic concepts connected with the general assumptions of a simple-system model, and a number of specific concepts connected with the particular assumptions adopted in the process of empirical implementation, or application, of a simple-system model. The *basic concepts* are: SYSTEM$_1$, conceived as a complex set of interrelated elements making up a separate whole and standing in specific relationships with the environment; FUNCTION$_1$, conceived as the contribution of a given element to the attainment or maintenance of some selected state of the other elements in the same system; and ELEMENT, conceived as any realistically or only nominalistically distinguished part of the system. The *specific concepts* of the simple functional analysis are: reciprocity, exploitation, consensus, conflict, dependence, autonomy, isolation, and structural context.

The reconstruction of the conceptual models presupposed by simple functional analysis will enable us to appraise the utility of this approach, as well as its limitations, by checking the degree of fit that characterizes the model of a simple system with respect to social reality; i.e., the subject that the model is supposed to represent. This critical examination of the model is taken up in Part III of this volume.

Chapter 7

DIRECTIVE
FUNCTIONAL ANALYSIS

The Model of a Teleological System

The model of a simple system I have been discussing thus far may be called primary because it includes the minimum set of assumptions adopted of logical necessity by any and every functional analysis. But functional analysis is often more complex than this, and supplementary assumptions are added to those of the simple system. Ascending the hierarchy of more and more complex, and, consequently, more and more restrictive, conceptual models, we come to the model of a teleological system.

The model of a teleological system contains two additional general assumptions. The particular mode of action characteristic of the system is defined as the directive organization. And the particular internal mechanism of the system underlying its mode of action is defined as self-regulation.

The assumption of directive organization describes the behavior of a system from an external point of view (sometimes referred to as the black-box approach). Attention is focused on the characteristics of the system as a whole, as opposed to the characteristics of its internal "anatomy and physiology." In the way of a preliminary definition, it may be said that a system is considered as directively organized if and only if in the repertory of its global states some may be distinguished as preferred; i.e., attained or maintained more often than could be expected on the basis of randomness. This is equivalent to saying that a directively organized system displays the tendency to attain some particular global states or to preserve these states when attained, and this despite the changes within the system itself and within its environment. This is of course an extremely general account of directive organization. To explicate this assumption, I propose to distinguish three component assumptions that constitute it.

The first component assumption is that of a *process*. The "behavior" of a system is conceived as a sequence of changes or transformations the system undergoes through time; it results in a causally interconnected chain of global states of the system, one state replacing the other. The assumption of a process is clearly implied by the notion of preferred states, or goal states, or simply goals of the system. By a goal is here meant just the end state, the point of destination, or the last state in the chain of states. The relevant question concerning the goal conceived as an end state, rather than an intended state, is not "whose goal?" but "the goal of what?" And the answer imposes itself: the goal of the specific process.

The second component assumption defines the process as *directive*. Now, the directiveness of a process amounts, as it seems, to two easily observable properties. First, that state of the system which is described as a goal is the last state of the system in that interval of transformations which is analyzed with respect to the goal in question. When the system enters this goal state the process under consideration is concluded. Second, that state of the system which is described as a goal does not occur at any earlier stage of the process; no element in the causal sequence of states is identical with it. Both properties of the directive process (sometimes also referred to as a teleological process) are emphasized by Mace (1949), who observed that there are:

> Three features of interest in the teleological process: (1) It is evoked by a negative condition E' and is such that the introduction of a contrasting condition E, at any time in the sequence would terminate the process in question. (2) It is such that . . . any action which increases the degree of E tends to be continued or repeated, whilst any action which decreases the degree of E tends to be discontinued. (3) It is such that with repetition of the process constituent actions which favor E tend to be stabilized whilst actions which are adverse to E tend to be eliminated, with the result that the process as a

whole approximates to a form in which it consists of a set of component actions performed in a certain order, which (a) performed in that order are sufficient to produce E and (b) are such that the omission of any action would prevent the occurrence of E [p. 535].

The third component assumption defines the process as *plastic*. The plasticity of the process may also be reduced to three easily observed particular properties. First, it is assumed that a given goal can be attained from various starting points or, in other words, that a given goal-directed process can be initiated by various events. Second, it is assumed that the process is relatively independent of variable external circumstances (at least within a certain range) or in a more metaphorical language, that a process will stubbornly strive for its goal state despite various obstacles provided only that these obstacles do not become unsurmountable. Thirdly, it is assumed that the process will "strive for its goal" through various causal sequences, or to use a metaphor again, by different roads. To sum up, the process that is marked by a large number of possible starting points, a relatively large degree of independence from external, changing circumstances, and by a large number of alternative paths leading to the goal state will be called plastic. This interpretation owes much to a discussion of purposeful activity in living organisms found in Russell (1945). In his account, the plasticity of the process acquires primary importance: "What is most characteristic of directive action is to strive stubbornly for its goal, use alternative means toward the same end, and achieve results in the face of difficulties [p. 110]."

The assumption of directive organization may be specified in a more formal and precise manner by outlining the main points of an explication made by Braithwaite (1960). All three partial assumptions I have distinguished are implicit in this discussion. Braithwaite starts with the notion of a causal chain of events c in the system b, which is nomically determined both by the initial state e of the system and by the extrasystemic variables, or field conditions, f. Then he defines the goal-attaining property of this chain by emphasizing that it ends in a certain selected event of a goal type, without containing any other event of this type. The third crucial notion is the variancy of the field conditions in which a system of the type b, with a given initial state e and a given goal state, will display the property of goal attainment. Braithwaite points out that there are three analytic possibilities: either the variancy has no member, and so there is no way to attain a goal state by this specified system, or the variancy has only one member, and so there is only one, strictly predetermined way of attaining a goal for that system, or—and this is the most interesting case—the variancy has more than one member "so that the occurrence of any one of alternative sets of field conditions is, together with *e*, sufficient for the attainment of a goal of type *G* [p. 330]." The last case is defining for the plastic or teleological chain of events or states.

The assumption of self-regulation describes the behavior of a system from an internal point of view (which is sometimes referred to as a translucid-box approach). Attention is focused on the "molecular" characteristics of system elements and their interrelations, and especially the ways in which they can account for the directive mode of system's "molar" transformations. In metaphorical terms, one is looking for the built-in mechanism that "pushes" the system toward its goal in spite of changing external circumstances, or "keeps" the goal state once it has been attained.

In the way of a preliminary definition, it may be said that a system is considered to be self-regulating if and only if it contains the compensatory mechanisms that enable it to preserve a preferred goal state (or a trend of development leading to a goal state) despite a relatively wide class of changes in the system's environment. The elements of a system are here bound together in such a manner that in the case of initial change in one of the elements (or the particular class of elements), the remaining ones spontaneously undergo compensatory changes, bringing the system back to the preferred state (or to the preferred trend of development). There are three conditions that are necessary to trigger the self-regulating mechanism: (*a*) the initial state must belong to the class of preferred states, or it must be a necessary phase in the causal chain of development leading to the preferred state (the self-regulating mechanism is always relative to a given selected class of states, the system that would be self-regulating with respect to all conceivable states is impossible by definition); (*b*) the initial change must be strong enough to throw the system out of the preferred state; (*c*) the initial change must not overrun the limits of compensatory abilities of the given system.

This general characteristic may be rendered more precise and rigorous. The most complete formal explication of the self-regulatory mechanism has been given by Nagel (1956, 1961). His analysis, which is by now a classic, may be briefly summarized as follows. Let *S* stand for any system, *E* for its environment, and *G* for the state of the system as a whole. To simplify matters, Nagel assumes that E remains unchanged in all its essential aspects, so that its effect on the occurrence of G in S may be disregarded. He further assumes that three of the elements of S: A, B, and C, can have an essential effect on the occurrence of G in S. The states of these elements are symbolized respectively as Ax, By, Cz. By substituting numerical constants $1, 2, 3, \ldots n$, for the variables x, y, z, one can indicate the values of the "state-variables" of these elements at a given moment. The state of S in those respects which are essential for the occurrence of G in S, can at every moment be described as some definite value of the matrix (Ax, By, Cz).

Each of the state-variables can take on different values, provided that these values be confined to a certain range determined by the nature of the element to which the variable refers. Thus, the state-variables must remain within the limits of objectively possible values; in other words, they must belong, respectively, to the classes Ka, Kb, Kc of values. The objectively possible, definite values of the matrix (Ax, By, Cz) can be subdivided into two classes. One would include all those states of the elements of S whose joint occurrence determines the occurrence of G in S. Nagel calls them "the states causally effective with respect to G." The other would include all the remaining combinations of the state-variables of elements of S, the occurrence of which results in the lack of G in S. All such definite values of the matrix (Ax, By, Cz) might be termed the states causally ineffective with respect to G.

Next Nagel makes the assumption that at the moment t_0 the system S is in the initial state (A_0, B_0, C_0) which belongs to the class of states causally effective with respect to G. And then the state of element A changes, so that at the moment t_1, the new state of the system (A_1, B_0, C_0) is no longer causally effective with respect to G. Now, the system may be so constructed that if the value of the state-variable of A remains in a class Ka of values, which is a subclass of its objectively possible values, then the values of the remaining state variables By and Cz will undergo compensatory changes, such that the state of the whole system returns to the class of states causally effective with respect to G. If, in the case discussed here, the value A_1 belongs to the class Ka of compensable changes, then By and Cz take on the values B_1 and C_1 (in place of B_0 and C_0), and the resulting state (A_1, B_1, C_1) is again casually effective with respect to G. Thus, in spite of the fact that the initial change of A transforms the state of the total system into one which is ineffective with respect to G, this change itself results in compensatory changes in the state-variables of other relevant elements, such that the system returns to a state causally effective with respect to G.

The self-regulating system which is characterized by the structural properties discussed in the preceding paragraphs (a certain "anatomy") may be characterized also by particular dynamic properties (a particular "physiology"). Let us reconstruct the basic dynamic property of a self-regulating system, and only such a system, its fundamental "law of motion." If each of those states of S which are causally effective with respect to G are symbolized by i and the class of such states $(i_1, i_2, i_3, \ldots, i_n)$ as I, then the determining effect of each of these states on G can be defined according to the nature of that determination, either as a necessary condition $(\sim I \supset \sim G)$, or as a sufficient condition $(I \supset G)$. Now, the hypothesis that what is necessary or sufficient for bringing about G will occur in S under normal conditions can be accepted as true only if S is directively organized and self-regulating with respect to G. Thus, the laws of the type: $(\sim I \supset \sim G) \supset i_k$ and $(I \supset G) \supset i_k$; where $1 \leq k \leq n$, which may be called, in Hempel's (1965) terms, "the general self-regulation hypotheses," hold in a directively organized system only. This seems a correct formal symbolization of the hypothesis

> to the effect, that, within certain limits of tolerance or adaptability, a system of the kind under analysis will—either invariably or with high probability—satisfy, by developing appropriate traits, the various functional requirements . . . that may arise from changes in its internal state or in its environment. Any assertion of this kind, no matter whether of strictly universal or of statistical form, will be called a (general) hypothesis of self-regulation [Hempel 1965: 317].

Every system that fulfills both major assumptions, that of directive organization and that of self-regulation, will be termed a *teleological system*.

The adoption of the model of a teleological system instead of the simple-system model entails radically new research priorities. First, attention is focused on the system as a whole and its global states, especially preferred ones, to the neglect of particular elements and their intrasystemic relationships. Second, attention is focused on the relationships of the "part–whole" type, to the neglect of relationships of the "part–part" type. The brand of functional analysis characterized by the adoption of the model of a teleological system (whether explicit or implicit) and, consequently, by the research priorities just specified, shall be called *directive functional analysis*.

What is the essence of this type of functional analysis? In simplest terms it amounts to distinguishing certain elements (institutions, modes of social action, norms, values, etc.) within an entity conceived as a whole (society, culture) and examining to what extent these elements contribute to the attainment or maintenance of preferred states of the system. These states are defined in various ways as "structural continuity," "persistence" (Radcliffe-Brown); "integration," "existence" (Malinowski); "adjustment," "adaptation" (Merton); "equilibrium" (Parsons); etc. The analyst is not interested in the states of particular elements for their own sake, but only from the point of view of their systemic relevance, i.e., the part they play in keeping the system in certain of its preferred states, or in bringing the system to that state in the future.

The basic difference between simple functional analysis and directive functional analysis is correctly indicated by Beattie (1964):

> Functional explanation in social anthropology does more than merely demonstrate that different, apparently independent, modes of social behavior are causually connected in certain systematic ways. It looks also for their implications for institutional systems. This is the teleological content of functionalism. The accent is not only on the discovery of causal links, important though this is; it is also, and especially on the part which one mode of institutionalized behavior plays in a systematic and already conceptually prefigured complex of interlocking institutions. We are dealing with what may be regarded analytically as part–whole relationships [p. 55].

The effects of the presence (or activity) of a given element on the preferred states of the system as a whole are considered as the *functions* of that element. This meaning of function is not alien to anthropological functionalism. In one of his earliest works, Radcliffe-Brown (1922) defined function as "the effects of an institution [custom or belief] insofar as they concern the society and its solidarity or cohesion [p. 234]." He (Radcliffe-Brown 1952) elaborated this definition thus: "The function of any recurrent activity, such as the punishment of a crime, or a funeral ceremony, is the part it plays in the social life as a whole and therefore the contribution which it makes to the maintenance of structural continuity [p. 180]." This meaning of function is also to be found in modern anthropology. For Kluckhohn (1944), "a given bit of culture is functional insofar as it defines a mode of response which is adaptive from the standpoint of society and adjustive from the standpoint of the individual [p. 47]." Nevertheless, the most widespread use of this concept of function is to be encountered in sociology. In the famous "paradigm for functional analysis in sociology," Merton (1967) defined functions as "those observed consequences which make for the adaptation or adjustment of a given system [p. 105]." Martindale (1960) is inclined to define function in general terms as, "a system-determined and system-maintaining activity [p. 445]," and in more specific terms as an "equilibrium maintaining operation [1965: 154]."

The most precise definitions of the present meaning of function are given by philosophers of science. Emmet (1958) remarked:

> To talk about a "function", and not only about a "result", will be to consider the process with reference to a unitary system with a persistent structure. This assumption of an ordered context means that if we say that x has a function, we are in fact saying more than that x has the consequence y. It has the consequence y within a system the efficiency or maintenance of which depends (inter alia) on y [p. 47].

And, to close our list of illustrative definitions, let us consider the definition offered by Nagel (1956), which corresponds to the explication of self-regulatory mechanisms discussed previously.

> By the "function" of an item (or set of items) in S one may understand simply some trait G which that item succeeds in maintaining in S. The item can then be represented as a state co-ordinate for G, and its function is the preservation of G in S. In this sense of the word a function of an item is a role it plays in S [p. 268].

This is obviously a different concept of function from the one discussed in Chapter 6. To distinguish it, I shall identify it by adding the numerical subscript 2. So, to rephrase and refine the second definition of function, one may say:

The FUNCTION$_2$ of an element E in the system S is $G(S)$, where
1. E contributes to the attainment or maintenance of the state G of S.
2. G belongs to a class of preferred global states of S.

Directive functional analysis was widely implemented in empirical research. It will be shown that whenever functionalists have attempted to explain, and not only describe social phenomena, they have espoused the assumptions of a teleological-system model (or still more restrictive assumptions) through logical necessity. Namely, in all cases where the existence or persistence of an element in the system is explained by pointing to its functional contributions, the argument takes one of the following forms: (1) *Explanans:* (a) this element is necessary for the attainment of a state G in S; (b) system S is in a state G; therefore (c) *Explanandum:* this element is present in the system S; or (2) *Explanans:* (a) this element is functional for the system; (b) if the element is functional for the system then it will appear in the system; therefore (c) *Explanandum:* this element appears in the system. The first argument is clearly untenable because it conceives of a given specific element as a necessary, unexchangeable condition for a given preferred state of the system. In fact, there are always alternative elements that can fulfill any social or cultural function. Thus, the second type of explanation is used more often. And as the premise (b) it obviously contains the "hypothesis of self-regulation," a precise symptom that the system is conceived implicitly as a teleological one. Thus, all explanatory accounts of social phenomena—religion, magic, myth, ritual, incest taboo, social stratification—may be considered as examples of directive functional analysis (or still more complex types of functional analysis which will be discussed in subsequent chapters).

The widespread use of directive functional analysis has led some critics to consider it as the exclusive form of functional analysis and even to identify it with functionalism as such. In a recent appraisal, "functionalism is conceived of as the doctrine which asserts that all recurrent social activities have the function of maintaining the social system," and the term *functionalists* is reserved to denote "the collectivity of theorists who look upon society as a system, the maintenance of which is the function of recurrent social activities [Whitaker 1965: 127, 128]." These remarks are justified in the sense that in directive functional analysis, functionalism assumes, for the first time, an identity. Whereas simple functional analysis could be identified with sociological analysis as such, directive functional analysis is obviously a distinct approach. With respect to this type of functional analysis, Davis's (1959) argument would be totally misdirected. But, on the other hand, one must not equate this particular type of functional analysis with functional analysis per se.

The model of a teleological system opens up new opportunities for spelling out the particular assumptions referring to the structural properties of social reality; it creates a new range of internal variability within the systemic–functional model. There are five new dimensions of internal variability within the framework of a teleological-system model. I shall attempt to reconstruct 10 particular assumptions defining the extreme alternative values of structural variables, along each of these dimensions.

Universal Functionality versus Specific Functionality

Granted that elements of the teleological system contribute to the maintenance or attainment of certain preferred states by the system as a whole, the question arises: Do all of them contribute in the same manner? Two opposite answers may be distinguished. *The assumption of universal functionality* claims that all elements of the system contribute positively to the system's preferred states. *The assumption of specific functionality* claims that some elements of the system may certainly be positively functional, but others may be neutral or even detrimental to the system's preferred states.

The first assumption implies a homogeneous image of society in which there are no dispensable elements and no malfunctioning parts. Everything works in perfect harmony, bringing about the preferred states of the system, or maintaining them after being attained. From such an image it is a very close step to the assertion that whatever is, is good and necessary, for otherwise it would not exist.

This assumption was certainly accepted by Malinowski (1936): "The functional view of culture insists therefore upon the principle that in every type of civilization, every custom, material object, idea and belief, fulfills some vital functions, has some task to accomplish, represents an indispensable part within a working whole [p. 132]." This extreme position was a logical consequence of Malinowski's vehement criticism of the notion of cultural survivals, which were widely accepted in the anthropology of his time, and explained the persistence of cultural elements that had lost all cultural functions in a changed situational and historical context, but nevertheless continued to exist. In Malinowski's (1969) view, cultural elements may change their characteristic functions, but they always fulfill some function. There are no "functionless" elements in human culture.

> A horse cart, and even more so, a hansom cab, does not "fit" into the streets of New York or London. Such survivals, however, do occur. The horse cab appears at certain times of the day or night and in certain places. Is it a survival? Yes and no. If we were to treat it as the best and most rapid or cheapest means of locomotion, it certainly would be both an anachronism and a survival. It obviously has changed its function. Does this function fail to harmonize with present-day conditions? Obviously not. Such an antiquated means of locomotion is used for retrospective sentiment, as a "ride into the past"; very often, I am afraid, it moves where the fare is slightly intoxicated or else romantically inclined [pp. 28–29].

The adoption of the assumption of universal functionality has rather unhappy research implications. The important questions of whether a given element fulfills any functions, and what kind of functions it does fulfill, are removed from the domain of empirical confirmation or refutation and settled in an a priori manner. The only valid question that remains is: What is the content of the function fulfilled by the given element, to what global preferred states does it contribute? This seems an undue and unfounded restriction of the field of empirical inquiry, for, as Merton (1967) correctly observed: "Although any item of culture or social structure may have functions, it is premature to hold unequivocally that every such item must be functional [p. 85]." This is obviously a question that should be open to empirical determination.

Due in part to Merton's searching criticism, the assumption of universal functionality has been abandoned in modern functionalism and replaced by the assumption of specific functionality. This assumption entails a more heterogeneous image of society in which some elements contribute to the maintenance or attainment of the society's preferred states (they are functional), some are irrelevant in this respect (they are functionally neutral), and some prevent or hinder the attainment or maintenance of preferred states (they are dysfunctional). These three possibilities are defined by Merton (1967):

> Functions are those observed consequences which make for the adaptation or adjustment of a given system; and dysfunctions, those observed consequences which lessen the adaptation or adjustment of the system. There is also the empirical possibility of non-functional consequences, which are simply irrelevant to the system under consideration [p. 105].

Let us specify a little more rigorously the concepts of dysfunction and functional neutrality. As I will attempt to show, the concept of dysfunction has at least three different meanings. To signify the meaning that appears in the context of the present assumption, I shall apply the numerical subscript 1. The other two meanings will be discussed in the context of more complex systemic–functional models. Thus, to rephrase and render more exact the first notion of dysfunction, one may say:

The DYSFUNCTION$_1$ of an element E in the system S is non-G (S), where
1. E contributes to the attainment or maintenance of the state non-G of the system S.
2. G belongs to the class of preferred global states of S (and thus non-G is the state opposite to the one preferred).

In a similar manner, one can also refine the notion of the functional neutrality of an element:

The NEUTRAL FUNCTION of an element E in the system S is $D(S)$, where
1. E contributes to the attainment or maintenance of the state D in the system S.
2. D does not belong to the class of preferred global states of S (and thus is simply different state, and not opposite to G).

It hardly needs stressing that the assumption of specific functionality is preferable, from a methodological point of view, to that of universal functionality. It directs empirical research to the assessment of the net distribution of elements within the system with respect to their functional roles. The determination of the dominance of functional, dysfunctional, and neutral elements in a given system at a given moment may be extremely valuable for explaining the present state of that system, as well as for predicting its future state (or the course of its development). The situation in which the majority of elements is functional seems especially conducive to social stability, the second, to social change, and the third situation signifies a state of indeterminancy in which the system is particularly vulnerable and responsive to all influences coming from the environment. To quote Merton (1967) once again:

> Far more useful as a directive for research would seem the provisional assumption that persisting cultural forms have a net balance of functional consequences either for the society considered as a unit, or for subgroups sufficiently powerful to retain these forms intact, by means of direct coercion or indirect persuasion. This formulation at once avoids the tendency of functional analysis to concentrate on positive functions and directs the attention of the research worker to other types of consequences as well [p. 86].

Uniform Functionality versus Diverse Functionality

The second dimension of variability within the model of a teleological system is a little different from the previous one. It is no longer concerned with the distribution of elements in the system according to their functions (or dysfunctions), but rather focuses on the balance of consequences of a given single element for the system as a whole. Two opposite solutions of this problem may be distinguished. *The assumption of uniform functionality* claims that a given single element has an unambiguous role in the system; it may be either functional, dysfunctional, or neutral, but can never perform all three roles. *The assumption of diverse functionality* claims that one and the same element may be both functional, dysfunctional, and neutral for the system or for various of the system's global preferred states; thus, there is always a net balance of consequences that a given element has for the system considered globally.

The first assumption seems characteristic of early anthropological functionalism. When the goal state of the system was defined in singular terms, as "survival," "persistence," etc., there was hardly any possibility for one and the same element to be at the same time contributing to, and working against, that state. Although the assumption of uniform functionality was never made explicit, it seems implicit in the works of Malinowski and Radcliffe-Brown, as well as some later anthropologists.

Only when the goal states of the system were defined in a more sophisticated manner, as a class of preferred states, rather than a singular state, did there appear the analytical possibility of an element's being functional for one of the preferred states, but dysfunctional or functionally neutral for others. This possibility was emphasized by Nagel (1956):

> Just as the claim that a given change is functional or dysfunctional must be understood as being relative to a specified G (or sets of G's), so the claim that a change is nonfunctional must similarly be construed as being relative to a specified set of G's. The change that is indifferent relative to G_1, may be functional, dysfunctional or non-functional relative to G_2 [p. 269].

It is well to notice that in the context of the present assumption, the concept of dysfunction acquires its second, distinct meaning, different from the one discussed earlier. It may be identified by the numerical subscript 2, and defined thus:

The DYSFUNCTION$_2$ of an element E in the system S is non-G_1 (S), where
1. E contributes to the attainment or maintenance of the states non-G_1, G_2, G_3, . . . G_n of the system S.
2. G_1, G_2, G_3, . . . G_n constitute the class of preferred global states of S.

In the first of its meanings, the concept of dysfunction entailed the simple recognition of the possible negative role of an element in the system. In the second meaning attention is called to the possibility of the negative and positive roles of the same element.

The assumption of diverse functionality has very important research implications. It requires the precise determination not only of the system with respect to which a given element is analyzed as functional, dysfunctional, or neutral, but also of the particular state of the system, out of the class of its preferred states. This necessitates in every case a complex relativization of functional analysis: to the particular system and to the particular state of the system—an important step in the direction of greater empirical specificity and greater operational significance of functional analysis. And it gives to functional analysis much greater explanatory and predictive power. The appraisal of the net functional consequences of a given element allows one to determine its role in the system as a seat of stabilizing, or, on the contrary, dynamizing tendencies. This seems crucial in explaining the system's present state, as well as predicting the direction of its development.

Equipotent Functionality versus
Differential Functionality

The third particular question that requires solution within the model of a teleological system refers to the relative force of functional (or, for that matter, dysfunctional) influences exerted on a given preferred state of the system by various elements. Two opposite answers may be distinguished. *The assumption of equipotent functionality* claims that all elements of a system have equal importance for the maintenance or attainment of that preferred state of the system relative to which they are functionally effective. To put it otherwise, this means that of the two elements functional for a given state of the system, one is not more functional than the other; and of the two elements dysfunctional for a given state of the system one is not more dysfunctional than the other. *The assumption of differential functionality* claims that the degree to which functional (or dysfunctional) elements contribute to the attainment (or nonattainment) of a given preferred state of the system varies. Some elements are more important in this respect, and some are less important.

The first assumption, without being made explicit, seems characteristic of anthropological functionalism. It clearly underlies the image of a society in which all elements are reciprocally and mutually interdependent. Early functionalists were equally concerned with all kinds of phenomena, institutions, norms, values, modes of social behavior, etc., and had not the conceptual means for weighting the differential significances of some of them for a society as a whole. All elements were seen as interacting with all others, and neither the degrees of intensity, nor the foci of interactions, were distinguished. This was obviously an undue restriction of functional analysis.

In more sophisticated functionalism the assumption of differential functionality predominates. In the words of Gouldner (1959):

> The analyst must cope with the task of determining the differential contribution made by different system parts to the state of the system as a whole. In short, different system parts make different degrees of contribution to either the stability or the change of the system, and these need to be analytically and empirically distinguished [p. 265].

The same assumption is also emphasized by Buckley (1967): "Just because a number of variables are interrelated in a systemic manner does not necessarily mean that each is of equal weight in producing characteristic states of the system; any systemic variable may run the gamut from insignificance to overwhelming primacy [p. 67]."

The assumption of differential functionality entails a more complex image of society in which not only are some elements functional and some dysfunctional or neutral, but within the classes of both functional and dysfunctional elements, there exists a hierarchical ordering of elements with respect to significance. Some elements are seen as more vital than others for the system's maintenance, and some are seen as more vital than others for the system's change. The elements on top of both hierarchies, those which are most functional or most dysfunctional, constitute the foci of stabilizing and destabilizing tendencies, respectively. The assessment of differential functionality (or dysfunctionality) of various elements seems crucial for explaining the present state of the system and predicting its future state. Therefore, from a methodological point of view, the assumption of differential functionality must be considered as much more fruitful than that of equipotent functionality.

Functional Indispensability versus Structural Alternatives

The basic relation defining the character of the model of a teleological system is that of an element's contribution to the global state of the system as a whole. In attempting to specify this relation by means of the particular assumptions of the model, I have been dealing so far with the characteristics of elements, i.e., one of the relata (the other being the state of the system). The next logical step is to specify the relation of contribution itself. What does it mean that an element contributes to the state of the system? The first approximation to the answer would be: The element is causally effective with respect to that state. But this is clearly not a specific characteristic. Thus, as a second approximation, the question—What does it mean that an element is causally effective?—gives rise to two opposite particular assumptions.

The assumption of functional indispensability claims that a given element constitutes a necessary condition of a preferred state of the system; in other words, without that element, a preferred state of the system could neither be attained nor maintained. *The assumption of structural alternatives* claims that a given element is a sufficient condition (or even less rigorously, a favorable condition) of a preferred state of the system; that is, when that element is present in the system, the preferred state is attained or maintained (either unexceptionally or with a significant degree of statistical probability), but without that element, a preferred state may also appear in the system.

The first assumption is characteristic of anthropological functionalism, and particularly of Malinowski. The assumption that, "in every type of civilization, every custom, material object, idea and belief fulfills some vital function, has some task to accomplish, represents an indispensable part within a working whole [Malinowski 1936: 132]," appears both in his theoretical claims and empirical assertions. In the context of Malinowski's empirical studies this idea reappears often. Discussing the institution of magic Malinowski (1954) remarked: "Without its power and guidance early man could not have mastered his practical difficulties as he has done, nor could man advance to the higher stages of culture. Hence the universal occurrence of magic in primitive societies and its enormous sway [p. 90]." On the role of myth in primitive culture, Malinowski wrote: "Myth fulfills in primitive culture an indispensable function: it expresses, enhances and codifies belief; it safeguards and enforces morality; it vouches for the efficiency of ritual and contains practical rules for the guidance of man [p. 101]." In sociological functionalism the assumption of indispensability is encountered less often, but it is by no means absent. For example, in discussing the institution of the family and the incest taboo, Davis (1949) commented: "When we think of the family's functions, its peculiar structure, and its reciprocal sentiments and roles, we can understand why the prohibition of incest is absolutely indispensable to its existence as a part of social organization [p. 404]." And in their "theory" of stratification, Davis and Moore (1945), as we have seen, go to great lengths to substantiate the assertion that only the differential gratification of social positions can ensure the proper recruitment of the most able and skilled personnel and, consequently, that social inequality is an indispensable mechanism of social survival (see also Schwartz 1955).

The assumption of indispensability calls up an image of society in which all its structures (institutions, norms, values, modes of social action, etc.) are necessary for the society's existence and can neither be modified nor replaced. Probably the most interesting aspect of human society, the infinite variability of its institutions, ways of life, customs, values, norms of behavior, etc., is removed from the range of empirical comparative research. We are told that whatever exists is necessary *because* it exists—not the first instance of a tautology in functionalism. Instead of the empirical analysis of elements from the point of view of their systemic relevance, we are offered an empty presupposition.

For modern functionalism, the opposite assumption, that of structural alternatives, equivalents, or substitutes, seems much more characteristic. This assumption, which Merton (1967) considered a "basic theorem [p. 87]" of functional analysis, is spelled out by him in the following words: "Just as the same item may have multiple functions, so may the same function be diversely fulfilled by alternative items [p. 88]."

A good example of an analysis in which the notion of structural alternatives plays a central part is provided by Hoebel's (1954) study of primitive law. In one chapter he attempts to explain the relative absence of legal institutions among the Eskimo, by reference to alternative institutions that fulfill the same function for that particular society:

> The multitude of taboos are mostly directed to spirits of animals or their controlling deities in order to guard against conduct offensive or disrespectful to them. So comprehensive is the taboo system that the paucity of legal rules in Eskimo culture is in large part caused by the encompassing supernatural sanctions which dominate Eskimo social and political life. Magic and religion rather than law direct most of their actions. [p. 70].

Other examples of analyses drawing on the assumption of structural alternatives are abundant in the context of a critical debate over the Davis–Moore "theory" of stratification. One important line of criticism deals precisely with the possibility of structural alternatives to inequality, as the means of fulfilling the function of recruiting of adequate personnel for the network of social positions. As Tumin (1953) correctly remarked:

> There are a number of alternative motivational schemes whose efficiency and adequacy ought at least to be considered in this context. What can be said, for instance on behalf of the motivation which . . . we

latterly have come to identify as "intrinsic work satisfaction"? Or, to what extent could the motivation of "social duty" be institutionalized in such a fashion that self-interest and social interest come closely to coincide? Or, how much prospective confidence can be placed in the possibilities of institutionalizing "social service" as a widespread motivation? . . . Admittedly, historical experience affords us evidence we cannot afford to ignore. But such evidence cannot legitimately be used to deny absolutely the possibility of heretofore untried alternatives [p. 391].

Let me define a little more rigorously the concept of structural alternatives (sometimes also referred to as structural equivalents or substitutes):

An element E_1 is a STRUCTURAL ALTERNATIVE with respect to the state G of the system S, where
1. The presence (or activity) of E_1 is a sufficient or favorable, but not necessary, condition of attainment or maintenance of G in S.
2. E_1 belongs to the nonempty class E of elements (E_1, E_2, E_3, . . . , E_n), each of which is a sufficient or favorable, but not necessary, condition of attainment or maintenance of G in S.
3. G belongs to the class of preferred states for the system S.

The scope of the class of structural alternatives, mentioned in the second defining premise, is of course limited. There is always a given empirical range of possible structural alternatives which is determined by the particular features of the society in question—by its internal constitution, as well as by external, environmental circumstances. This is emphasized by Merton (1967) in his category of "structural constraint." A good empirical example is provided by Holt (1965), who pointed to the specific circumstances that precluded the development of governmental institutions in the Dinka society as an alternative to the informal, diffused means of social control embedded in the kinship and religious structure at the moment of Nuer conquest: "The existing social structure of the Dinka social system blocked the development of these new social structures that one would predict would emerge as the result of changes in the environment [p. 107]." He specifies these particular structural features in some detail.

The assumption of structural alternatives has very important research implications. It directs attention to the tremendous variability of structural arrangements which may fulfill the same function, and so it makes the research worker aware of the wide range of possible cultural and historical diversities. In cases where a certain expected structure is lacking in a given society it requires the search for structural alternatives and, in this way, helps to disclose the latent functions of some other existing institutions. And where a certain expected structure is present in a given society, the assumption requires the search for particular factors to explain the absence of other equally feasible alternatives.

Equilibrium versus Disequilibrium

The last aspect left for further specification by the general model of a teleological system refers to the characteristics of the system's preferred states. The general assumptions of the model postulate that the system has a tendency to maintain a preferred state, and, consequently, in case of any disturbance of that state, some internal compensatory mechanisms are called into play to restore the preferred state. But within the model of a teleological system, nothing at all is posited with respect to the particular properties of that preferred state. This point must be especially emphasized because of the common charge to the effect that the model of a teleological system has, of itself, strong static implications, that it assumes the spontaneous restoration of the status quo. The point is that the preferred states that are restored need not be construed in static terms. The general assumption claims only that a system has a tendency to attain or maintain a certain preferred state; it does not specify that state. The criticism of a static bias directed against the general model of a teleological system is totally unfounded and results from the confusion of two distinct levels of analysis: the level of the general assumption and the level of particular assumptions. Two alternative particular assumptions referring to the properties of the preferred state are equally possible within the framework of the model, and only one of them actually involves the static bias.

The assumption of equilibrium claims that the preferred state (or the class of preferred states) for a given system (or a system of a certain kind) is given and predetermined once and for all. It is described in an absolute, and not relative, manner as a particular configuration of state-variables or elements and their interrelations. This particular configuration or, in other terms, this particular structure of the system, is seen as tending to be preserved by self-regulatory mechanisms. To quote Buckley (1967), who discussed this assumption under the heading of *morphostasis:* "It refers to those processes in complex system–environment exchanges that tend to preserve or maintain a system's given form, organization or state [p. 58]."

The assumption of disequilibrium, on the other hand, claims that the preferred state of the system (or the class of preferred states) is itself changing. It is determined in a relative manner as a particular type of relationship between the system and its environment. This particular relationship tends to be preserved by self-regulatory mechanisms and precisely by virtue of these self-regulating processes the system's internal structure may be modified or even totally transformed. Keeping the relation between system and environment intact by definition indicates the necessity of structural changes in the system when the environment itself changes. Buckley (1967) refers to this type of self-regulating processes by the name of *morphogenesis:* "It will refer to those processes which tend to elaborate or change a system's given form, structure or state [p. 58]."

The first assumption is predominant in the works of functionalists, and particularly within that type of functionalism sometimes referred to as "normative functionalism" (cf. Lockwood 1964: 244). It is probably left over from the organic analogy and the consequent attempt to determine certain constant points within society in order to assess the functions of social elements. Such a reference point is found in the common normative structure, the institutionalized order of norms and values. The full internalization of a common normative structure by the members of a society is considered as the preferred state, and any tendency to deviate or any actual deviance from that order, arising from extrasystemic sources, meets with "automatic" reactions to restore the previous order. The mechanisms most often mentioned in this context are socialization and social control, which operate by means of various sanctions. The tendency to preserve the given normative order is "very generally expressed in the concept of equilibrium [Parsons and Shils 1951: 180]." The equilibrium in question is of a particular kind. It may be called a "stable equilibrium"—the condition in which "the variables of the system are in such a relationship to each other, that all remain constant in values, not by assumption but by their interaction [Hagen 1961: 146]." The characteristic position of normative functionalists is aptly summarized by Krupp (1965): "The system moves toward a given state of equilibrium and restores this state when it is disturbed. The desired state of equilibrium is identified as the system's goal [p. 70]."

The alternative assumption of disequilibrium is actually uncommon in functionalist writings. Some suggestions pointing in this direction are put forward by Cancian (1960), who claims that the terminal (preferred) states of the system need not be singular, predetermined in absolute terms, but may well consist of a series of states succeeding each other in a regular cycle or sequence. In this case, what is preferred is not so much a particular state, but rather a certain path of change that the states of the system are following. A similar idea is found in the concept of dynamic, or moving, equilibrium which is defined by Hagen (1961) in the following way: "If one or more of the parameters of a system goes through a process of continuing change . . . the values of the variables at which they are in equilibrium may be expected to change continuously. We may then refer to a moving equilibrium [p. 147]." The most explicit recognition of this assumption may be encountered in Nagel's (1956) attempt to formalize certain aspects of functional analysis:

> A system S may exhibit at different times a series G_1, G_2, . . . G_n of mutually incompatible G's, which succeed each other because of certain "built in" features of S or because of certain progressive changes in E [environment] or both. The double problem then would be to (1) ascertain the order of the succession of the G_i's with the aim of formulating their law of development, and (2) discover the state-coordinates which control the development [p. 281].

The image of society invoked by the assumption of disequilibrium is quite different from the previous one. If the preferred state of the system is not fixed, but regularly changing, the structural conditions of the maintenance or attainment of preferred state will be changing, too. With the change of the preferred state, the structural conditions causally effective with respect to the old state, become causally ineffective, or even dysfunctional with respect to the new one. The self-regulating compensatory mechanisms tend to restore the situation in which the actual structural conditions would be again causally effective with respect to the system's preferred state. In the self-regulating process, these mechanisms bring about the modification or even the total transformation of the structure. But exactly at the moment when the new structure is brought into being, the preferred state of the system has already changed again, and the whole cycle of structure elaboration and transformation begins anew at a higher level. There is a constant, necessary lag between the new preferred state and the old structural arrangement. The typical state of the system is thus an eternal disequilibrium which is being constantly, but never ultimately, overcome. This constant process of structural change is brought about by regular changes in the system's environment or by changes inside the system which modify the relation of the system to its environment. The modification of this relation then triggers the self-regulating mechanism.

The diverse research implications of both the assumption of equilibrium and that of disequilibrium are best seen in the context of a specific problem. I will take the analysis of a social normative system, i.e., prevailing norms and values of different types, as an illustrative example. If one applies the assumption of disequilibrium to the analysis of the institutionalized normative structure of a social system, it will appear much less homogeneous and consistent. All elements will be seen to be in a continuous process of change, and so, at any given moment there will be some elements that remain from the former structure, some that are proper to the present preferred state of the system, and some that anticipate the future restructuring of the system. Various strains, contradictions, and conflicts on the normative level are the natural results of this situation. Yet all this is dismissed as residual in the context of the assumption of equilibrium. This basic point of difference between both assumptions, as concerns their research implications is well argued by Buckley (1967):

> The equilibrium theorist . . . typically points out that there are, in any society, sets of more or less common norms, values, expectations, and definitions of the situation supported by sanctions of one kind or another. However, he equally typically fails to mention that every society of any complexity also has a quite stable set of alternative, diverse, deviant, or counter norms, values, etc., as well as a vast area of ambiguities and uninstitutionalized "collective" behavior of all shades and degrees. These can only be swept under the theoretical rug by definitional fiat; they are residual, or not really part of the system at all. But by this time, the argument has been reduced to word-play [pp. 10–11]

From a methodological point of view the assumption of disequilibrium seems to have obvious advantages over the assumption of equilibrium. It does not bring about the premature closure of the theoretical system and makes the research worker duly sensitive to the vast range of relevant empirical data.

The Conceptual Framework of Directive Functional Analysis

To recapitulate the conclusions of my argument, there are two additional general assumptions and five pairs of alternative particular assumptions that make up the model of a teleological system. These assumptions are logically presupposed in directive functional analysis.

In the context of a directive functional analysis some new concepts appeared, both basic—linked with general assumptions—and specific—linked with particular assumptions. In this way the language of functional analysis was significantly enriched.

The language of directive functional analysis contains three *basic concepts:* SYSTEM$_2$, conceived as a set of interrelated elements making up a separate whole and standing in a specific relationship with the environment, which reveals a pattern of directively organized transformations due to internal self-regulatory mechanisms; PREFERRED STATES (or goal states) of the system, conceived as the global properties characteristic of the system as a whole, which tend to be attained or maintained by the system despite the specific range of environmental or intrasystemic changes; and FUNCTION$_2$, conceived as the contribution of a given element to the attainment or maintenance of a preferred state of the system as a whole.

Within the framework set by the general assumptions, a variety of different particular solutions is possible. Their adoption introduces a series of *specific concepts* to the language of directive functional analysis. Among these, the most important are: *dysfunction$_1$, dysfunction$_2$, functionally neutral elements, structural alternatives, net balance of consequences, structural constraint, equilibrium, and disequilibrium.*

The utility of all these concepts for describing and explaining social reality depends on the fit of the conceptual models they presuppose to the studied domain of reality itself. If social reality (or some aspects thereof) can be considered as an adequate empirical interpretation of the model of a teleological system, then all the concepts listed above must be considered useful or even indispensable for its study. And, should they not prove so, they must be discarded. I shall suspend judgment for a while. The crucial issue of the empirical adequacy of systemic–functional models is taken up in Part III of this volume.

Chapter 8

FUNCTIONAL–REQUISITE ANALYSIS

The Model of a Functional System

The types of functional analysis discussed thus far do not exhaust the functional approach as such. Some more advanced types, based on more complex and consequently more restrictive conceptual models, are frequently encountered. The next in the order of growing complexity and restrictiveness is the model of a functional system.

The model of a functional system contains two additional general assumptions. One adopts the external point of view and describes the system's mode of action with no regard to its internal structure. The other supplements the picture by taking into account the internal mechanism responsible for the given mode of action. Both may be considered amplified versions of the assumption of directive organization and self-regulation. To emphasize this affinity I shall call them the assumption of double-level directive organization and the assumption of double-level self-regulation.

The assumption of double-level directive organization requires the distinction of two types of internal states within the system: global states, which are characteristic of the system as a whole, and partial states characterizing certain aspects of the system. Some partial states, like some global states, are preferred in the sense of there being a tendency to preserve them, which cannot be accounted for by pure randomness. The elements of the system contribute directly to the realization of preferred partial states, and in turn the realization of each of these partial states constitutes a necessary condition for attainment or maintenance of some preferred global states of the system as a whole. Thus, the causal chain linking the element and the system is broken into two phases, and the element's contribution to the system is considered as indirect, or mediated.

The partial preferred states, the reference whereby to assess the functions of each element, are called "functional requirements," "functional requisites," "functional imperatives," or simply the "needs" of the system.

The mode of action characteristic of the system construed in this manner may be described as double-level directive organization because the elements are supposed to have a tendency to attain or maintain the partial preferred states (to fulfill functional requirements, satisfy functional needs of the system, etc.), and the satisfaction of the system's needs contribtues to the attainment or maintenance of preferred global states (systemic goals). The property of directiveness characteristic of the processes occurring at both phases may be explicated in the same manner as was done in Chapter 7. In fact, as the processes are of the same kind, save for their more mediated character, there is no need to repeat the explication in detail.

The assumption of double-level self-regulation requires the distinction of two intrasystemic mechanisms responsible for the directive mode of the system's action. The first mechanism brings about the attainment or maintenance of partial preferred states (satisfaction of needs). It involves compensatory reactions, at the level of elements, which are brought into play when needs are not adequately satisfied. The second mechanism brings about the attainment or maintenance of global preferred states (goal achievement on the part of the system as a whole). It involves compensatory reactions, at the level of partial states, which are triggered when system goals are not satisfactorily achieved. In this case, systemic needs themselves may be modified (e.g., suppression of some needs on behalf of others, creation of new needs, elimination of those which cannot be satisfied under the changed circumstances, etc.), thus bringing the system back to its global preferred state. The general properties of the self-regulating mechanisms, as well as the limiting conditions of their effectiveness, are the same in both cases. They were explicated rigorously in Chapter 7, and therefore there is no need to repeat the points made there.

The adoption of the model of a functional system entails particular research priorities. First, attention is focused on the partial states of the system, and especially the preferred partial states ("requirements," "requisites," "imperatives," "needs," etc). Second, attention is focused on the relation of the elements to partial preferred states— "requisite-fulfillment," "need-satisfaction," etc. The type of functional analysis characterized by the adoption of the model of a functional system (whether explicit or implicit) and, consequently, by the research priorities mentioned here, shall be referred to as *functional–requisite analysis*.

What is the essence of this type of functional analysis? In simplest terms it consists of distinguishing certain elements (institutions, modes of social action, norms, values, social relationships, etc.) within an entity conceived of as a whole (society, culture) and examining to what extent these elements contribute to some preferred partial state (requirement, requisite, imperative, need) of the system as a whole. The analyst is not interested in the states of particular elements (the values of variables characterizing them) for their own sake, but only in terms of their systemic relevance. But, as Holt (1965) correctly emphasized: "There is a major problem of differentiating between the system-relevant and the nonrelevant effects of a structure [p. 88]." In the context of directive functional analysis, this problem is solved by stipulating certain global preferred states of the system (like "continuity," "integration," "adaptation," etc.) as the reference points for the functions of the elements. In the context of functional–requisite analysis this problem is solved by stipulating a certain set of functional requirements of the system as a measure of an element's functionality. To quote Holt (1965):

> We propose to make this distinction [between relevant and irrelevant effects of a structure] by equating system relevance with system requiredness. For any social system there is a set of functional requisites—operational conditions that must be satisfied if the system is to continue to exist . . . It is possible . . . to view various activities as contributing to the satisfaction of one or more of these requisites [p. 88].

In this case, it is neither the elementary state of some other element, nor the global state of the system, but rather a partial state of the system that constitutes the point of reference for evaluating the roles of individual elements in the system.

The effect of the presence (or activity) of a given element for the attainment or maintenance of the partial preferred states of the system (for need satisfaction or requisite fulfillment) is considered a *function* of this element. This concept of function is already present in the earliest works of functional anthropology, and particularly in theoretical statements as opposed to empirical research. To give an example, Malinowski (1969) presented a definition of function in the following terms: "Function means, therefore, always the satisfaction of a need from the simplest act of eating to the sacramental performance in which the taking of the communion is related to a whole system of beliefs determined by a cultural necessity to be at one with the living God [p. 159]." This is obviously a different concept of function from both concepts of it discussed heretofore. To distinguish it, I shall append the numerical subscript 3. Thus, to rephrase and make precise our third definition of function, one may say:

The FUNCTION$_3$ of an element E in the system S is $N_1 (S)$, where
1. E contributes to the attainment or maintenance of N_1 in the system S.
2. N_1 belongs to the class $N (N_1, N_2, . . . , N_n)$ of partial preferred states of the system S (it is one of its functional requirements).

The most symptomatic and easily recognizable feature of functional–requisite analysis is to be found, not in the explicit definition of function in these terms (which is rather rare), but rather in the use of terms such as "functional requirement," "functional requisite," "functional imperative," "need," and the like. The substantive content of partial preferred states qualified by these terms is very diverse. The common meaning of this crucial notion must therefore be sought among its formal properties. As a rule, the needs, requirements, etc., of the system are defined as such partial states each of which constitutes a necessary and indispensable condition for maintaining (or begetting) the system as a whole in one of its global preferred states (survival, adaptation, structural continuity, etc.) Let me quote some representative definitions of the relevant concepts. The notion of "cultural need" was defined by Malinowski (1969) in this way: "We can define the concept of basic needs as the environmental and biological conditions which must be fulfilled for the survival of the individual and the group [p. 75]." A group of functionally oriented sociologists (Aberle *et al.*, 1950) in an article intended to be the manifesto of the functionalist school defined the notion of "functional prerequisites" thus: "Functional prerequisites refer broadly to the things that must get done in any society if it is to continue as a going concern, i.e., the generalized conditions necessary for the maintenance of the system concerned [p. 317]." Levy (1952) couched his definition of "functional requisite" in similar terms:

> A functional requisite, as that term is used here, is a generalized condition necessary for the maintenance of the unit with which it is associated, given the level of generalization of the definition of that unit and the most general setting of such a unit [p. 62].

> In brief it may be said that a given function is a requisite of any society if in its absence the relationship between the unit under discussion and its setting in the most general terms . . . can be shown to be such that one (or some combination) of the four conditions for the termination of a society would result [p. 149].

And Bennett and Tumin (1964), in reviewing the general characteristics of some types of actions they consider to be the "cultural imperatives" of society, hasten to add: "These six classes of activities represent not only what various groups the world over actually do but, additionally, what these groups have to do if they are to survive and continue as human groups [p. 9]."

The common definitional criteria applied by all these authors should now be clear. Thus, to rephrase and render precise the definition of functional requirement, one may say:

The FUNCTIONAL REQUIREMENT of the system S is N, where
1. N is a partial state of the system S.
2. N is a necessary condition of attainment or maintenance of the state G in the system S.
3. G belongs to the class of global preferred states of the system S as a whole.

One comment is in order at this point. The concept of functional requirement could be conceived equally well in a different way, not as a necessary condition, but as sufficient condition or, even less formally, as a favorable condition of the G state of the system. It seems that most difficulties encountered in the empirical application of this concept stem from the restrictive definition formulated traditionally. A more liberal definition would give functional–requisite analysis more flexibility in dealing with social reality, of course, for the price of formal elegance. But, to the best of my knowledge, such an alternative concept of functional requirements has never been formulated in functionalist works.

The most elaborate catalogue of functional requirements was included in the so-called "theory of needs" worked out by Malinowski. Starting from the assumption that human culture has a basically instrumental character (i.e., provides the means for satisfying individual and social needs), Malinowski proceeds to the classificatory scheme in which particular needs are linked with certain "cultural answers" to them. This portion of Malinowski's work is highly praised by Parsons (1957), who, notwithstanding his generally critical attitude toward the founder of functionalism, considers it the most valuable contribution to the theory of social systems:

> There is with one exception no point at which Malinowski has more to teach us than one or several of his contemporaries or predecessors. The one exception to which I refer is the classification of the functional imperatives of "culture" and the responses to which they relate [p. 70].

> This, it can be said, is an authentic, if sketchy, classification of the functional imperatives of social systems [p. 65].

In Malinowski's (1969) view, the first group of needs has a biological character. They derive from the particular anatomical and physiological constitution of the human being as a particular type of biological organism. "All men have to eat, they have to breathe, to sleep, to procreate, and to eliminate waste matter from their organisms wherever they live and whatever type of civilization they practice [p. 75]." These needs are called "basic." Their catalogue, linked with specific cultural reactions, may be reconstructed as seen in Table 8.1.

Particular basic needs are satisfied by men in various ways depending on the concrete social and cultural circumstances in which they find themselves. In the process of satisfying basic needs, some new needs are created. These "derived needs" constitute the second major group. They are equally as significant as the basic ones: "Dependence on the cultural apparatus, however simple or complex, becomes the conditio sine qua non [Malinowski 1969: 121]." The catalogue of derived needs and cultural reactions linked with them may be reconstructed as seen in Table 8.2.

TABLE 8.1

Catalogue of Basic Needs Linked with Specific Cultural Reactions[a]

Cultural reactions (elements E of the system)	Basic needs (subclass of the class N of preferred partial states of the system)
1. Nutritive system	1. Food, nutrition
2. Kinship structures, family, schools	2. Reproduction, procreation, upbringing of children
3. Shelter, houses	3. Bodily comfort, necessary temperature, climatic conditions
4. Weapons, fortifications, army organization	4. Safety
5. Various activities, sports	5. Movement
6. Hygiene, therapy	6. Health

[a] Based on Malinowski 1969: 91.

The last group of needs is called "integrative." Malinowski is not very clear as to the meaning of this term, nor does he catalogue the needs so designated. It seems that he has in mind some necessary conditions of continuity of human culture and its transmission across generations. The elements that contribute to the satisfaction of these conditions are: language, verbal and written tradition, value systems, religion, magic, myth, art, etc.

TABLE 8.2

Catalogue of Derived Needs Linked with Specific Cultural Reactions[a]

Cultural reactions (elements E of the system)	Derived needs (other subclass of the class N of preferred partial states of the system)
1. Economic system	1. Production, utilization, and reproduction of the material apparatus
2. Political organization	2. Organization of collective activities, necessity of authority, leadership, power and sanctioning apparatus
3. Social control	3. Codification and regulation of human behavior by means of sanctions
4. Educational system	4. Transmission of acquired cultural heritage

[a] Based on Malinowski 1969: 125.

In sociological functionalism the concept of functional requirements has fundamental importance. Almost every author attempts to put forward his own list of partial states considered necessary and basic for the proper functioning of human society. Of the many such attempts, often arbitrary and ad hoc, I would like to discuss two in which there is some attempt made at rigorous derivation from some wider theoretical scheme.

A rather elaborate set of functional requisites is presented by Aberle and his colleagues (1950: 322). At the outset they determine four general conditions any one of which, if realized, could terminate the existence of society. These conditions are:

1. The biological extinction or dispersion of the members.
2. Apathy of the members (understood as the lack of motivation to take up any social action).
3. The war of all against all.
4. The absorption of society into another society.

As is easily to be seen these conditions are a simple reversal of the definition of society; they are analytic consequences of this definition. The authors go on to list some basic functional requisites defined by means of the four conditions listed above. "The performance of a given function is prerequisite to a society if in its absence one or more of the four conditions dissolving a society results [Aberle 1950: 323]." The full list of functional requirements understood in this sense may be reconstructed as in Table 8.3.

A very similar cataloguing of functional requirements is given by Levy (1952) in *The Structure of Society* (see pp. 149–97).

The most concise list of functional requirements was formulated by Parsons (1951) as a derivation from his fundamental idea of "pattern-variables." He elaborated the idea of the functional requirement thus:

> Societies are subjected to certain functional exigencies. . . . These exigencies are of two classes: first, the universal imperatives, the conditions that must be met by any social system of a stable and durable character, and second, the imperatives of compatibility, those which limit the range of coexistence of structural elements in the same society in such a way, that, given one structural element, such as a given class of occupational role system, the type of kinship system which goes with it must fall within certain specifiable limits [p. 167].

TABLE 8.3

Functional Requirements[a]

Functional requirements	Condition terminating society when relevant requirement not satisfied
1. Provision for adequate relationship to the environment and for sexual recruitment	1 or 4
2. Role differentiation and role assignment	2 or 3
3. Communication	2 or 3
4. Shared cognitive orientations	1 or 3
5. A shared, articulated set of goals	2 or 3
6. The normative regulation of means	2 or 3
7. The regulation of affective expression	3
8. Socialization	1 or 2 or 3 or 4
9. The effective control of disruptive forms of behavior	3

[a] Based on Aberle 1950: 323–330.

In regard to specific imperatives, Parsons asserted: "It is possible to reduce the essential functional imperatives of any system of action, and hence of any social system, to four, which I have called pattern-maintenance, integration, goal-attainment and adaptation [1965a: 38]." One may reconstruct Parson's catalogue as seen in Table 8.4.

The Parsons's AGIL scheme has been extensively discussed in the literature. In the context of the present discussion it serves mainly illustrative purposes, and hence I will disregard all the intricate, theoretical, methodological and even philosophical problems that it generated.

The model of a functional system adds three new dimensions of structural variability to those previously discussed. New choices as to the values of variables along each of those continuous dimensions are necessary. Possible alternative extreme choices will be reconstructed as three pairs of particular assumptions.

Monofunctionality versus Multifunctionality

The first particular question that arises within the model of a functional system has to do with the relation of elements and the functional

TABLE 8.4

Relation between Elements and Functional Requirements[a]

Type of structural element (classes of elements E specialized in satisfying a given requirement)	Functional requirements (N states of the system)
1. Socialization, social control	1. Pattern maintenance: maintenance of conformity to the prescriptions of the normative system
2. Economic sectors of a social system; both in macroscale and in microscale (e.g., in the household)	2. Adaptation: activities that provide mobilizable resources
3. Political sectors of a social system; both in macroscale and in microscale	3. Goal attainment: maintenance of desired relationships with the environment. Organization and manipulation of actions for that objective
4. Symbolic, ritualistic, expressive forms of providing for identity feelings	4. Integration: maintaining the identity of the system and the attractiveness of its goals for the participants

[a] Based on Holt 1965: 93; Boskoff 1957: 220–221; Bredemeier and Stephenson 1962: 42.

requirements of the system. This question may be phrased in the following way: Is any element functionally relevant (functional, dysfunctional) with respect to one, and only one functional requirement, or can it satisfy several functional requirements, either simultaneously or at different moments? To put it otherwise: Are the elements of the system strictly specialized in meeting functional requirements, or are they more flexible in this respect?

The assumption of monofunctionality claims that there is a close correspondence between functional requirements and the particular structures (elements) that satisfy them. This correspondence is not considered mutual, but rather as unidirectional; it is admitted that one and the same requirement may be satisfied by several elements (alternatively or in conjunction), but at the same time each given element is supposed to be oriented toward one and only one requirement. *The assumption of multifunctionality*, sometimes also referred to as *the assumption of multiserving structures* (cf. Hernes 1971: 40), claims that each element has several functions, satisfying various functional requirements.

The first assumption is typical of early anthropological functional-ism. Here, the attempt to correlate a given institution with a particular need is most pronounced. As Merton (1967) commented: "This in-volves a concept of specialized and irreplaceable structures . . . [p. 87]." But if the relationship between a given structure (element) and a given functional requirement is conceived as a one-to-one corre-spondence, then obviously the element is implicitly defined by its function, and the assertions referring to the relations of given elements and given requirements are devoid of any empirical meaning (are analytic and not contingent). Functional–requisite analysis changes into an exercise in building tautologies.

This unfortunate research implication is avoided through the adop-tion of the assumption of multifunctionality. It is explicitly posited by Merton (1967): "The same item may have multiple functions [p. 87]." The specification of functions served by a given element is left for empirical research. Of course the possibility of specialized structures is not excluded: "The structures of a unit, however they may be differentiated, may and do have differing orientations and emphases . . . [Levy 1952: 65]," but neither is the possibility of flexi-ble, unspecialized structures. The structures (elements) and the func-tional requirements are defined independently, and so the assertions referring to their mutual relations obtain empirical meaning; they are no longer tautological or analytic, but become empirical and con-tingent. The second assumption seems typical of modern sociological functionalism, where the correspondence between structures and func-tions is never postulated a priori, but rather is empirically determined.

Commensurate Requirements versus
Contradictory Requirements

The second question implied by the model of a functional system refers to the mutual relations of the functional requirements them-selves, and may be spelled out in this way: Are these partial preferred states of one and the same system necessarily commensurate, or are they sometimes contradictory?

The assumption of commensurate functional requirements claims that the attainment by the system of a particular preferred partial state (the satisfaction of one of its functional requirements) does not in any way diminish the chances for attainment or maintenance of other preferred partial states (the satisfaction of other functional requirements). *The assumption of contradictory functional requirements* claims that the attainment by the system of some of its preferred partial states may significantly hinder the attainment by this system of some other preferred partial states.

The first assumption implies an image of society in which the satisfaction of functional requirements harmoniously contributes to the attainment or maintenance of the global preferred state (society's persistence, continuity, adaptation, integration, etc.). The second assumption implies the image of society in which the necessary conditions of global preferred states are themselves contradictory. Hence, the attainment or maintenance of such a state is brought about only at the cost of conflicts, contradictions, and competition as to the priorities in satisfying functional requirements in view of the scarcity of resources available to a system.

It is easily seen that the assumption of commensurate functional requirements, at the level of a functional system, corresponds closely to the assumption of consensus at the level of a simple system; likewise does the assumption of contradictory functional requirements correspond to the assumption of conflict, at the level of a functional system. Both assumptions constitute extensions of basically the same images of social reality.

The first assumption seems typical of early functionalism. In modern sociological functionalism, the second assumption is explicitly posited by Sjoberg (1967)[1]:

> Our fundamental premise is that all social systems are, at one time or another, plagued by contradictory functional requirements (or imperatives) and that these are associated with the formation of mutually antagonistic structural arrangements that function to meet these requirements [p. 340].

> A social system is an exceedingly complex entity whose structural arrangements, reflecting mutually antagonistic functional demands upon it, are often at odds with one another [p. 341].

A very good example of contradictory functional requirements is provided by Levy (1952):

> It is quite conceivable . . . that a given condition (or pattern) be at one and the same time necessary for the maintenance of a system

---

[1] Originally published as Contradictory functional requirements and social systems, by Gideon Sjoberg and reprinted from the *Journal of Conflict Resolution.* Vol. IV, No. 2 (June 1960) pp. 198–208 by permission of the publisher, Sage Publications, Inc.

and to some degree dysfunctional to it. For example, mass production
in a highly industrialized society is necessary for its maintenance, but
the process involved may so upset the members as to "predispose"
or "motivate" them to seek outlets in extremist, highly authoritarain
political faiths . . . that may well prove to be incompatible with the
maintenance of a highly industrialized society [p. 87].

Thus, the functional requirements of industrial society may well
be seen to be: (*a*) to maintain mass production, and (*b*) not to
maintain mass production.

Obviously, both assumptions entail opposite research priorities; the
first focuses attention on consensual, harmonious relations, the second,
on conflictual and contradictory relations. In different empirical contexts each may appear an adequate tool for analysis. But it seems
that the usefulness of the second assumption for the analysis of
modern, complex societies exceeds by far the usefulness of the first
assumption.

Constant Requirements versus Changing Requirements

The last question implied by the model of a functional system
refers to the characteristics of each functional requirement by itself
and may be specified thus: Are the partial preferred states of the
system (functional requirements) predetermined, given once and for
all, or rather can they themselves change through time?

The assumption of constant functional requirements claims that
for a system of a given type the list of functional requirements is
fixed and may be specified without regard to the particular circumstances of time, place, situation, etc. *The assumption of changing
functional requirements* claims that what is necessary for the attainment of the system's preferred global states depends on the wider
changing environment in which the system is situated, and hence
some partial state which is a functional requirement at a given moment
may well lose this character at some other moment. And, of course,
a given partial state may acquire the character of a functional requirement (preferred state) under changed environmental conditions.

The first assumption invokes an image of society as a static system
with a fixed set of requirements. The second assumption invokes the
image of a dynamic system in which the requirements themselves
are changing. It is obvious that at the level of a functional system,
the first assumption is the extension of the assumption of equilibrium
as posited at the level of a teleological system, and the second assump-

tion is the extension of the assumption of disequilibrium. They constitute aspects of two opposite images of society. All that was previously
said in favor of the second image (conflict–contradiction–disequilibrium) applies mutatis mutandis in the present context.

The assumption of constant functional requirements is deeply rooted
in the tradition of functionalism. But in modern functionalism the
assumption of changing requirements has gained recognition, too.
It is explicitly posited by Levy (1952): "The functional requisites
of a unit may be different if the definition of the unit remains unchanged but the setting of the unit changes [p. 40]." In somewhat
different terms the same point is made by Hernes (1971): "One must
ask not only what causes changes within a homeostatic variable, but
also what tends to cause changes between homeostatic variables, such
that one is substituted for another [p. 27]."

The Conceptual Framework of
Functional–Requisite Analysis

To recapitulate the conclusions of my argument: There are two
additional general assumptions and three pairs of alternative particular
assumptions that make up the model of a functional system. These
assumptions are logically presupposed by functional–requisite analysis,
the third type of functional analysis that has been distinguished.

In the context of functional–requisite analysis some new basic and
specific concepts appeared. In this way the language of functional
analysis was significantly enriched.

The language of functional–requisite analysis contains three *basic
concepts:* SYSTEM$_3$, conceived as a set of interrelated elements making
up a separate whole and standing in a specific relationship with the
environment; a system with a pattern of directively organized transformations, both with respect to global preferred states and to partial
preferred states (functional requirements), due to the internal self-
regulatory mechanisms operating both at the level of the system as
a whole and at the level of some particular partial sets of elements;
FUNCTIONAL REQUIREMENTS of the system, conceived as partial states
of the system necessary for the attainment or maintenance of its global
preferred states; and FUNCTION$_3$, conceived as the contribution of a
given element to the attainment of partial preferred states of the
system (or the satisfaction of its functional requirements).

Within the framework set by the general assumptions, a variety of different particular solutions is possible. Their adoption introduces a series of *specific concepts* to the language of functional–requisite analysis. The most important among these are: *monofunctionality, multifunctionality, commensurate requirements, contradictory requirements, constant requirements,* and *changing requirements.*

The discussion of the empirical adequacy of the model of a functional system, i.e., the closeness of fit between the model and social reality, appears in Part III of this volume.

FUNCTIONAL–MOTIVATIONAL ANALYSIS

The Model of a Purposeful System

The models discussed thus far have a defect in common which is particularly serious when the models are applied in the analysis of societies. The model of a simple system, the model of a teleological system, and the model of a functional system do not take into account the properties of the elements constituting the system, but focus exclusively on the structure of the total system and its mode of functioning. Yet there is a nontrivial respect in which the human beings acting in a society differ from wheels, pinions, cells, and tissues considered as elements of mechanic and organic systems. The basic difference amounts to the fact that human beings are themselves directively organized and self-regulating entities. As biological organisms they are directively organized and self-regulating with respect to certain preferred organic states like health, continuity of life, etc. But this is not the whole story. What is still more important, as conscious organisms they are also directively organized and self-regulating with respect to certain purposes; i.e., they are able to define certain states as wished for or valuable and adjust their behavior accordingly. Emmet (1958) made this point quite clearly:

> It is characteristic of human beings as distinct from the parts of physiological organisms and servo-mechanisms, to have purposes (however

misguided) as well as functions (however useful) [p. 105]. . . . I suggest therefore, that we need to consider a social activity not only in functional terms, asking: "What does this activity effect in interrelation with other activities in some system taken as a whole?" but also in purposive terms, asking: "What are these people trying to do?" [p. 107].

This is a qualitatively new property of the system. It is taken into account in the next model in our hierarchy of increasing complexity and restrictiveness—the model of a purposeful system.

To my knowledge, at the level of formal, rigorous considerations, the definition of this model has not yet been accomplished. From the traditional individualistic point of view, it is the theory of decisions that leads in this direction, and from the traditional holistic point of view, general systems theory, information theory, and cybernetics. The construction of the synthetic formal model combining the merits of both individualistic and holistic approaches without their one-sidedness, would certainly be a very significant achievement in terms of social analysis. Such a model, and only such a model, could represent adequately the irreducible specificity of society, which seems to rest on the fact that society is composed of people, as well as the irreducible specificity of the human individual, which arises from the fact that he is a member of society. In the absence of the formal elaboration of this model, I must restrict my remarks to a rather loose and general characterization.

The model of a purposeful system adds two general assumptions to those that have been listed previously. The first refers to the characteristics of the elements, the second, to the relationship between elements and with the whole.

The assumption of purposeful rationality claims that a large part of human action is consciously oriented to the achievement of certain purposes. The individual has a conscious idea of the purpose and the program of behavior supposedly relevant to achieving it, and the behavior is constantly modified according to the perceived degree of the attainment of the purpose. To put it otherwise, such actions are consciously selected which, in view of the actor's knowledge and accepted norms (values), seem to lead most directly to the most preferred results (purposes) in any given circumstance. This property of human action is widely recognized by functionalists. To quote Levy (1952): "Man as an animal is capable of conscious teleological action. That is to say, men consciously seek to bring about a state of affairs which at least in theory, from the actors' point of view would be different in some degree if they did not orient their actions to a particular goal [p. 174]."

The factor of purposeful rationality bestows upon human beings all the characteristic features of self-regulating systems. What is specific for this sort of a self-regulating system is the possibility of orienting behavior not only to goals which objectively are attainable, but also to goals which objectively are unattainable. The idea of something which from an objective point of view cannot be achieved has in this specific case a definite causal influence on the course of human behavior.

The assumption of integration of individual purposes and systemic goals claims that there is a wide class of individual purposes the attainment of which is the condition (either sufficient or necessary or only favorable) of the attainment or maintenance of the preferred states of the system as a whole (whether global or partial). The realization of his purposes by the acting individual is in this case relevant to the satisfaction of the functional requirements of society, or for the direct realization of system goals (global preferred states). In such a case, in the individual's acting purposefully toward his private goals, he contributes also to the goals of society. As Goode (1951) observed: "Human beings strive to realize their own purposes, but doing so they also contribute to the needs of society [p. 38]." Individual purposes of this type, whose realization is a conditioning factor with respect to the satisfaction of functional requirements, or the attainment or maintenance of the preferred states of society as a whole, shall be referred to as *sociocentric purposes*. This term is roughly equivalent to what Levy (1952) called "the basic value or goal orientations of the society" and defined as "the goals that are such that the member of a given society must hold them sufficiently in common to 'motivate' the performance of the functional requisites of that society . . . [p. 175]."

The model of a purposeful system entails the reorientation of research priorities. The focus of attention turns to the individual and his motivations and especially to the degree to which his actions are system relevant and system determined.

What is the essence of *functional–motivational analysis?* In simplest terms it consists of distinguishing certain individual actions (or patterns of actions) and examining to what extent these elements contribute to the realization of sociocentric purposes of the individuals involved, and hence, indirectly, to the satisfaction of functional requirements or the attainment of global preferred states by the system. The analyst is interested in individual actions exclusively from the point of view of their relevance to the system. But the immediate reference point for the evaluation of the functions of any given action is neither the state of some other element in the system, nor the system's global state, nor the functional requirements of the system, but rather a particular class of individual purposes held by the acting individuals; namely, the sociocentric purposes.

In the context of functional–motivational analysis, the concept of function again acquires new meaning. By *function* is here meant the effect of a given activity on the realization of sociocentric purposes by the individual. This meaning will be identified by the numerical subscript 4. To rephrase and make precise the fourth definition of function, one may say:

The FUNCTION$_4$ of the activity A of an individual I who acts in the system S is $P(I)$, where
1. A is a means for attainment of P (contributes to the attainment of P).
2. P belongs to the class of sociocentric purposes of the individual I (P contributes to the attainment or maintenance of the functional requirements or global preferred states of the system S).

This is undoubtedly the version of functional analysis that is least frequently encountered. Some hint of this approach is given in Malinowski's work; for example, in discussing magical and religious activities, he points out the ways in which the realization of individual purposes simultaneously contributes to the stability of society (1954: 26). Similarly, describing totemism and its role in primitive economy, he appeals to psychological forces determining the attitudes of primitive people toward animals as sources of food. These principles operating on the individual level explain some actions which are functional for the society as a whole. But the concept of FUNCTION$_4$ is not elaborated in his works, presumably because of the more general deficiency of his approach; namely the lack of an adequate theory of human motivation that could provide a bridge between his theory of systemic needs and the analysis of social institutions (or social actions) responding to these needs.

In sociological functionalism an attempt to develop the methodologi-

cal principles of functional–motivational analysis was made by Bredemeier (1955). In the article on "Methodology of Functionalism" he
states five procedural rules which in my opinion come close to the
codification of this specific type of functional analysis:

> (1) Productive analysis begins with a statement of the kind of action
> necessary to maintain some system of inter-relationships. . . . (2) It
> states the motivational conditions necessary to produce that action (the
> normative criteria of gratification which will yield the relevant action).
> (3) It describes the motivational patterns actually operating so as to
> produce the uniformity under analysis. (4) It seeks to find the source
> of those patterns (to isolate the normative criteria responsible for the
> observed actions). (5) It compares the consequences of the operating
> motivations with the motivations described as necessary. . . . (6) It
> finally assesses the role played by the uniformity in question in contribut-
> ing to the system of which it is a part [p. 180].

In the course of analysis prescribed by Bredemeier one can distinguish three phases. The first, covered by the first and second rules,
amounts to the reconstruction of those individual actions and motivations which are necessary for the satisfaction of functional requirements, or the attainment of preferred global states in the system as
a whole. Assuming that these actions are consciously purposive and
rational, this phase is equivalent to the determination of sociocentric
purposes that are relevant to the given social system. The second
phase, covered by the third and fourth rules, amounts to the descrip-
tion of actual activities taking place within the system, as well as
actual purposes that are revealed by these activities (whether sociocentric or not). The third phase, covered by the fifth rule, amounts
to the evaluation of actual activities in terms of the reconstructed
ideal of purely sociocentric activities.

The model of a purposeful system opens up new dimensions of
structural variability, and hence new possibilities for particular assumptions defining the properties of social reality. I shall attempt
to reconstruct six particular assumptions defining the extreme, alternative values of structural variables along three dimensions of variability.

Sociocentric versus Egocentric Images of Man

The first structural problem has to do with the ratio of sociocentric
purposes to all purposes held by individuals in a given society and,

particularly, the ratio of sociocentric purposes to egocentric (i.e., system indifferent or even system detrimental) ones. *The assumption of sociocentrism* claims that the majority of individual purposes is essentially sociocentric; there is a close fit between those states of affairs that the members of society want to achieve and those states of affairs which are favorable from the point of view of systemic goals. According to Wrong (1961), this assumption is inherent in the dominant image of man characteristic of contemporary sociology, namely the "oversocialized conception of man." Parsons (1951) espouses the assumption of sociocentrism quite explicitly when he claims that the characteristic feature of the social system is "the integration of a set of common value patterns with the internalized need-disposition structure of the constituent personalities [p. 42]." The sociocentric image of man easily leads to the dismissal of a whole array of empirically significant problems dealing with individual and collective deviations.

The assumption of egocentrism claims that the majority of individual purposes is egocentric in essence, i.e., either irrelevant to, or dysfunctional for, the society as a whole. To put it otherwise, there is almost no fit between those states of affairs that individuals attempt to achieve and the states of affairs that would be favorable for the system. Certainly, such an image of man is also one-sided, and perhaps unduly pessimistic. To rephrase Wrong, one could call it "the unsocialized conception of man." It is obvious that both assumptions may be useful in different contexts for conceptualizing different research problems, and their ultimate adequacy must be determined case by case, by means of empirical research.

Intended versus Unintended Functions

The second problem that has to be solved within the model of a purposeful system has to do with the relationship of the functions of a given activity (conceived in objective terms) and the intentions or motivations of the acting individual. These are obviously separate categories. The function is always some kind of objective result. The concept of function relevant in the present context, FUNCTION$_4$, signifies the objective, actual consequences of some activity for the sociocentric purposes of the individual. There must exist the objective causal nexus between the given activity and the state of affairs defined by an individual as his purpose in order to speak of functions in this sense. On the other hand, the notion of intention or motive is purely subjective. It signifies the individual's ideas concerning his purposes, as well as the effective means to attain them. These ideas may have no counterpart in reality. To mix up the objective and subjective aspects of activity would constitute a gross mistake. Unfortunately, sociologists are often guilty of this confusion. As Merton (1967) observed, in sociological literature there is often "the inadvertent confusion . . . between conscious motivations for social behavior and its objective consequences. Our scrutiny of current vocabularies of functional analysis has shown how easily, and how unfortunately, the sociologist may identify motives with functions [pp. 114–15]."

But even distinguishing clearly between both aspects of activity, one may still want to know what is their relationship. And specifically one may ask about the subjective qualification of objectively functional activity. What intentions or motivations brought about this activity? What kinds of rationalizations or justifications are devised for the activity? Are the purposes supposedly realized by a given activity congruent with its actual, objective functions? All these questions are relevant in terms of the complete characterization of a given activity.

The assumption of intended function claims that there is a close correspondence between the individual's intentions (what he wants to achieve) and the functions of his activity (what he actually achieves). The image of the goal that motivates a given activity and the goal that is attained as the result of that activity are the same. This assumption invokes an extremely simplified and, one might say, unduly optimistic, picture of society. As Merton (1967) has pointed out very emphatically:

> It need not be assumed, as we shall presently see, that the motives for entering into marriage ("love," "personal reasons") are identical with the functions served by families (socialization of the child). Again, it need not be assumed that the reasons advanced by people for their behavior ("we act for personal reasons") are one and the same as the observed consequences of these patterns of behavior. The subjective dispositions may coincide with the objective consequences, but again, they may not. The two vary independently [p. 79].

The class of objective consequences or functions of a given activity is in some cases wider than the class of intended consequences, in some cases it is narrower (this will be a case of unsuccessful actions), and in some cases both classes may be simply exclusive.

These possibilities are acknowledged in *the assumption of unintended functions*. This assumption claims that the subjective intentions and the objective functions of a given activity are often inconsistent. What one wants to achieve often has little or nothing to do with what one's activity actually achieves.

This assumption was implicitly accepted by Malinowski (1969). In his analysis of social institutions, he distinguished six constitutive elements that they contain: charter, personnel, norms, material apparatus, activities, and function. "Organized on the charter, acting through their social and organized cooperation, following the rules of their specific occupation, using the material apparatus at their disposal, the group engages in the activities for which they have organized [p. 53]." And, on the relationship between charter and function, Malinowski wrote: "Finally we have introduced the concept of function, that is, the integral result of organized activities, as distinguished from charter, that is, the purpose, the traditional or new end to be obtained. The distinction is essential [p. 53]." The assumption of unintended functions can often be uncovered in Malinowski's analysis of magic, myth, and religion. For example, in his interpretation, the subjective intentions of the participants in a funeral rite include: the expression of deference to the dead and his family, the assurance of favors for him and his family on the part of the deity, etc. On the other hand, the objective consequences (functions) of the same activity are quite different; it provides the community with standardized, routinized, and commonly accepted modes of overcoming a crisis, it releases stress, asserts the solidarity of the group, and in this way serves both the persons immediately involved and the community as a whole.

In contemporary anthropology the assumption of unintended functions is widely recognized. To quote one example, Spiro (1961), in his study of the relationship between the social structure and personality, made explicit this assumption: "Acts have intended and unintended functions. That is, the consequence of an act may be the consequence which was intended by its performance, or it may be one which was not intended by its performance [p. 107]."

And in sociological functionalism the same assumption was introduced by Merton (1967) in his famous paradigm for functional analysis. He considers it crucial to distinguish "those objective consequences for a specified unit (person, subgroup, social or cultural system) which contribute to its adjustment or adaptation and were so intended" from the "unintended and unrecognized consequences of the same order [p. 117]."

The assumption of unintended function seems much more fruitful from a methodological point of view. It opens up new avenues of empirical inquiry. The search for situations in which people's intentions do not coincide with the effects of their activities may prove crucial for the analysis of society. It may reveal the real mechanism and the real operation of the social system, as opposed to the ideal of such a mechanism and operation held by the actors.

Manifest versus Latent Functions

The second subjective qualification of individual activity has to do with the perception of consequences that the activity brings about, whether or not those consequences are intended or unintended. It is obviously not the same to be aware of such consequences and to intend them. Both may vary independently. This notion was apparently rejected by Merton (1967), for whom there is a one-to-one correspondence between the aspect of perception and the aspect of intention. Both aspects are fused in his definition of manifest and latent function: "Manifest functions are those objective consequences contributing to the adjustment or adaptation of the system which are intended and recognized by participants in the system; latent functions, correlatively, being those which are neither intended nor recognized [p. 105]." I suggest construing the relevant concepts in a narrower sense, relating the distinction between manifest and latent functions only to the aspect of perception or awareness of objective consequences brought about by a given activity on the part of acting persons. Thus, *the assumption of manifest functions* would claim that the acting individual is usually aware of the consequences of his actions for the system as a whole, whether the consequences are immediate or remote. And *the assumption of latent functions* would claim that the consequences of the activities for the system are rarely, if ever, recognized by the members of society. This narrower meaning of the categories is explicitly accepted by Spiro (1961):

> If manifest functions are those consequences of role performance which are recognized by the members of society, latent functions are those

consequences which—whether intended or unintended—are not recognized. That the paradox of an intended but unrecognized function is apparent rather than real, becomes clear when one considers that motives may be unconscious, as well as conscious [p. 108].

The assumption of latent functions was explicitly adopted by Davis (1949): "The actor's perception of the world is so limited in countless ways that he cannot know all the consequences of his behavior. The latter may therefore have functions which he in the pursuit of his ends does not see." And, he adds: "Some of the ends that are farthest from any knowledge that a social function is being performed are of the greatest functional importance [p. 125]." It seems that this assumption was also adopted very early by anthropological functionalists in their empirical "field studies." In Hernes's (1971) view the assumption of latent functions constituted one of the major postulates of anthropological research: "A major point of many functional analyses in anthropology and sociology has been to show that various social mechanisms or structures have been maintained not for their expressed purpose but for their latent, unrecognized consequences for other homeostatic variables [p. 37]."

The conceptual distinctions between intended versus unintended and manifest versus latent functions seem to have considerable importance for empirical sociological research. Following Merton (1967), one may list four arguments in support of them. First, these distinctions "clarify the analysis of seemingly irrational social patterns [p. 118]." For example, the problem of persistence of prejudices, magical rituals, and more generally, all irrational types of activities may be best comprehended in terms of their unintended and latent functions. Second, these distinctions "direct attention to theoretically fruitful fields of inquiry [p. 119]." When a sociologist starts to probe beyond the intended and manifest consequences of behavior into its varied, and rarely recognized, effects, he is apt to encounter the problems that are most important for him qua sociologist. Third, "the discovery of latent functions represents significant increments in sociological knowledge [p. 122]" precisely because these functions are excluded by definition from the realm of common sense knowledge. The specific contribution of the sociologist to knowledge of human society may be most sought in this area. The unintended and latent functions are the proper subject of scientific inquiry. Fourth, the discovery of such functions "precludes the substitution of naive moral judgments for sociological analysis [p. 124]." The evaluation of every activity or institution requires the appraisal, not only of "good or bad intentions" which brought it into being, but also and in the main, the whole complex of remote, long-range, and diversified consequences, usually unintended and latent.

A good example of an empirical analysis in which both pairs of distinctions were used is provided by Melford Spiro (1961) in his studies of the Melanesian community of Ifaluk. In discussing magic rituals, which among primitive peoples have presumed therapeutic significance, he distinguished six different functions: (*a*) intended and recognized personal function (defeat of bad ghosts); (*b*) intended and recognized personal function (emotional security); (*c*) unintended and recognized social function (solidarity of the group); (*d*) intended and unrecognized personal function (reduction of stress and hostilities); (*e*) unintended and unrecognized social function (deflection of aggression from society, outlet for hostilities); and (*f*) unintended and unrecognized social function (cohesion of the community) (see Spiro 1961: 113–14). This example gives some idea as to the potentialities of the distinctions drawn in this section.

The Conceptual Framework of Functional–Motivational Analysis

To recapitulate the conclusions of my argument: There are two additional general assumptions and three pairs of alternative particular assumptions that make up the model of purposeful system. These assumptions are logically presupposed by functional–motivational analysis, the fourth type of functional analysis that has been distinguished.

In the context of functional–motivational analysis some new concepts appeared; these were both basic—linked with general assumptions—and specific—linked with particular assumptions. In this way the language of functional analysis was significantly enriched.

The language of functional–motivational analysis contains three *basic concepts:* SYSTEM$_4$, conceived as a set of interrelated elements each of which is directively organized and self-regulating with respect to the wide class of purposes; SOCIOCENTRIC PURPOSE, conceived as such and only such a purpose held by the individual, the realization of which purpose contributes to the attainment or maintenance of preferred states (global or partial) of the system as a whole; and

FUNCTION₄, conceived as the contribution of a given activity to the realization of the sociocentric purposes of an individual.

Within the framework set by the general assumptions a variety of particular solutions is possible. Their adoption introduces a series of *specific concepts* to the language of functional–motivational analysis. Among these, the most important are: *unintended function, intended function, manifest function,* and *latent function.*

The issue of the empirical adequacy of the purposeful-system model is discussed in Part III.

Chapter 10

FUNCTIONAL–SUBSYSTEMIC ANALYSIS

The Model of a Multiple System

Previously I had considered simple, teleological, functional, and purposive systems to be single entities, and my analysis of them focused on the internal aspects of each system, i.e., on the elements located within the system's boundaries, as well as their intricate interrelations and varied states. The next, and final, elaboration of the systemic–functional model amounts to viewing the systems in their plurality and taking into account their, so to speak, external relationships with other systems. The set of assumptions that allows for this perspective will be called the *model of a multiple system.*

The model of a multiple system contains three additional general assumptions. The first focuses on the number of systems, the second on the kinds of systems, and the third on their mutual interrelations.

The assumption of plurality of systems states simply that the subject matter under study may be adequately represented only by a set of variously interrelated systems. They may either be equivalent, construed on the same level, or hierarchical, construed on different levels. In the second instance one of the systems may be considered as a subsystem of the other.

The assumption of heterogeneity of systems states that the systems included in the model are both formally and substantively varied:

formally, because they may belong to the different categories distinguished earlier—they may be simple, teleological, functional, or purposeful. Substantively they may vary because they may include different types of elements, these elements may be bound together in various relationships, and the characteristic preferred states of each (whether elementary, partial, or global) may be distinct.

The assumption of boundary interchange states that there are definite relationships binding all the systems together. In an operational sense this means that any changes in elementary, partial, or global states of one of the systems have definite consequences with respect to the elementary, partial, or global states of the other systems. In some cases, there is also a sort of mutual interpenetration of the systems; the elements of one being simultaneously the elements of the other.

The adoption of the model of a multiple system carries with it particular research priorities. First, attention is focused on the delimitation of the several subsystems within the wider whole, and the definition of relationships both among them and between each of them and the whole. Second, the frame of reference for the evaluation of functions performed by a given element is not only the subsystem in which it is directly involved, but also the other subsystems which it influences indirectly, across the subsystem's boundaries. The type of functional analysis characterized by the adoption of the model of a multiple system (whether explicit c: implicit) and thus by the research priorities mentioned here shall be called *functional–subsystemic analysis.*

What is the essence of this type of functional analysis? In simplest terms it amounts to distinguishing certain elements (institutions, modes of social action, norms, values, social relationships, etc.) within an entity conceived as a subsystem of a broader system, and examining to what extent these elements contribute to the attainment or maintenance of elementary, partial, or global preferred states of the other subsystems in the same system. The analyst is not concerned with the states of particular elements for their own sake, but rather is interested in their impact on the other subsystems of the system. It is not the state of some particular element, nor the preferred state of the system as a whole, nor functional requirements, nor sociocentric purposes, but rather any of these in all the relevant subsystems that constitute the reference point for evaluating the role of a given element.

In the context of functional–subsystemic analysis, the concept of function acquires a new meaning. By *function* is here meant the contribution of an element included in one system to the attainment or maintenance of certain preferred states in another system (or systems). This definition of function was clearly suggested by Ackerman and Parsons (1966): "A function is an energic output of an action system into another system, controlled informationally by the adaptive mechanism of the receptor system. . . . Of course an analyst may be interested in intrasystemic interchanges; in such a case, the term 'subsystem' is substituted for the term 'system' [p. 31]." To distinguish this meaning of function from the meanings previously specified, I shall identify it by the numerical subscript 5. Thus, to rephrase and make our fifth definition of function precise, one may say:

The FUNCTION$_5$ of an element E of the system S is (R or G or N or P)(S_i), where
1. E contributes to the attainment or maintenance of the state R or G or N or P of the system S_i.
2. R, G, N, and P are selected preferred states of the system S_i (elementary, global, partial, or individual).
3. S_i is any member of a class (S_1, S_2, . . . S_n) of the sub-systems of S or systems different from S, but linked with it by determinate relationships.

The differentiation of several subsystems within the broader social reality is nothing particularly new in the history of sociology. The image of social reality as complex and heterogeneous is certainly one of the basic tenets of sociology. But functionalists attempt to clarify these distinctions, and what is even more important, to incorporate them into a common frame of reference, to derive them from definite theoretical presuppositions.

The most elaborate attempt of this kind is to be found in the works of Parsons (1965a):

Most empirically significant sociological theory must be concerned with complex systems, that is, systems composed of many subsystems [p. 30].

A complex social system consists of a network of interdependent and interpenetrating subsystems, each of which, seen at the appropriate level of reference, is a social system in its own right, subject to all the functional exigencies of any such system relative to its institutionalized culture and situation and possessing all the essential structural com-

ponents, organized on the appropriate levels of differentiation and
specification [p. 44].

The whole of the highest order, in my terms, the multiple system,
Parsons has called, "the system of action." It contains four separate
subsystems: the cultural system, the social system, personality, and
behavioral organism. Their differentiation is based on the role they
play in the system of action. The essential function of the cultural
system in the system of action consists of pattern maintenance; the
essential function of the social system is integration; the essential
function of personality is goal attainment; and the essential function
of the behavioral organism, adaptation.

Parsons has applied the same criteria of differentiation at a lower
level of generality. Thus, four subsystems are distinguished within
the social system. They are: a social control subsystem providing
for the functional requirement of pattern maintenance; a societal community subsystem providing for the function of integration; a political
subsystem providing for the functional requirement of goal attainment; and an economic subsystem providing for the functional requirement of adaptation. Parsons goes to great lengths to describe the
interrelations between the subsystems at several levels of generality.
The central conceptual category describing the interrelation between
the cultural and social systems is construed as the institutionalization
of normative patterns. The other concepts relevant to the analysis
of the relationships between subsystems include internalization and
socialization, referring to the processes of personality formation under
the influence of a given social and cultural setting. As a result, Parsons
(in Ackerman and Parsons 1966: 33) attempts to produce "a picture
of vibrant systems in sensitive interpenetration of each other, stimulating and responding to each other, linked and made lively by the
flow of energy, controlled and regulated by information."

The second example of an explicit elaboration of a multiple-system
model may be found in the works of Kluckhohn (1962). In his analysis
of the concept of culture, he distinguishes four dimensions of each
act of behavior. The first is the biological aspect. Here human behavior
is the same as animal behavior. The second is the social aspect, taking
into account the intricate interrelations of individual acts in the network of interactions. The third is the cultural aspect, which focuses
attention on the specific ways and means by which behaviors are
carried on in a given community. The fourth is the individual aspect,

which denotes all the idiosyncracies typical of the behavior of a particular human being. Kluckhohn (1962) emphasizes the intricate links
between all four aspects. It does not seem contrived to consider these
three aspects as subsystems of a larger behavioral system.

Within the model of a multiple system there arise new possibilities
of structural variability. The decisions as to the value of variables
along each of the structural dimensions are provided by the particular
assumptions. There are four particular assumptions of this kind, and
they may be presented as two pairs of alternative extreme cases.

Functional Unity versus Functional Disunity

The first decision that has to be made concerns the relationship
between the element and the several subsystems of the same system.
Are the relationships similar in each case or are they different?

The assumption of functional unity claims that "standardized social
activities or cultural items are functional for the entire social or cultural system [Merton 1967: 79]"; i.e., a given element is equally functional for all the subsystems of that system. The same is true of dysfunctional activities or elements. *The assumption of disunity* claims
that one and the same element may have various functions with respect to different subsystems of the system of which it is a part.

The first assumption is accepted by Malinowski (1954) in the context of his empirical analyses. To illustrate this one may quote his
study of religion in which he equates the functions of ritual for the
personality subsystem with the functions of the same ritual for the
social subsystem: "We have seen already how religion, by sacralizing
and thus standardizing the other set of impulses, bestows on man
the gift of mental integrity. Exactly the same function it fulfills also
with regard to the whole group [p. 53]."

The assumption of functional unity, considered as one of the three
"prevailing postulates of functional analysis," is subjected to specific
criticism by Merton (1967). He suggests *the assumption of disunity*
as more useful empirically:

> We have observed the difficulties entailed in confining analysis to
> functions fulfilled for "the society," since items may be functional for
> some individuals and subgroups and dysfunctional for others. It is
> necessary, therefore, to consider a range of units for which the item
> has designated consequences: individuals in diverse statuses, subgroups,
> the larger social system and culture systems. (Terminologically, this

implies the concepts of psychological function, group function, societal function, cultural function, etc.) [p. 106].

It is worth noting that the assumption of functional disunity invokes a concept of dysfunction that is distinct from the two that were explicated earlier. I shall identify this new meaning by the numerical subscript 3. The third concept of dysfunction can be defined in the following way:

The DYSFUNCTION$_3$ of an element E in the system S is non-$(R_1$ or G_1 or N_1 or $P_1)(S_1)$, where
1. E contributes to the attainment or maintenance of the state non-R_1 or non-G_1 or non-N_1 or non-P_1 of the system S_1.
2. R_1, G_1, N_1, and P_1 are the preferred states of the system S_1 (elementary, global, partial, and individual).
3. S_1 belongs to the class S_1 of the subsystems of S or systems different from S, but linked with it by determinate relationships.

In its first meaning, the concept of dysfunction implied the simple recognition of the negative role of an element, in the second meaning is called attention to the possibility of the same element's playing negative and positive roles with respect to different preferred states of the same system (it required the relativization of the concept of function to the specific state); in the present meaning, it focuses on the possibility of the same element's playing negative and positive roles with respect to the preferred states of different systems or subsystems (it requires the relativization of the concept of function to the specific system or subsystem). Similarly, there is the empirical problem of determining the net balance of consequences (functional and dysfunctional) that a given element may have for the various subsystems of a certain system to which it belongs (cf. Nagel 1956: 272).

The assumption of functional unity and the assumption of functional disunity imply opposite images of society and consequently have opposite research implications. The second assumption seems to have decisive advantages over the first from a methodological point of view. It is more fruitful for empirical research, and gives functional analysis far greater explanatory and predictive powers. All that was explained away by a priori postulation in the context of the first assumption is open to empirical investigation and is considered as problematic. The appraisal of the net balance of functional consequences of a given element for various subsystems allows the determination of its role in the system as a seat of stabilizing or activating tendencies. This seems crucial for explaining the system's present state, as well as for predicting its development. On the other hand, the appraisal of the net balance of consequences that various elements have for every subsystem allows the determination of the subsystems most likely to be changed and, thus, the loci of future restructurings of the whole system, as well as the subsystems most likely to be preserved, i.e., those exhibiting conservative tendencies.

Subsystemic Integration versus Subsystemic Disintegration

The second dimension of variability within the model of a multiple system concerns the relationships between separate subsystems within the wider whole of the given system. Are the relationships between subsystems consistent and harmonious or inconsistent and antagonistic? *The assumption of subsystemic integration* claims that the attainment or maintenance of preferred states in one of the subsystems does not lessen the chances for attainment or maintenance of preferred states on the part of other subsystems. *The assumption of subsystemic disintegration* claims that the resources which can be mobilized by the system in order to keep its subsystems in preferred states are limited; consequently, the allocation of resources to one subsystem withholds resources from the others. Thus, the attainment of preferred states by one of the subsystems hinders the attainment of preferred states by other subsystems.

The first assumption seems implicit in traditional, and especially anthropological, functionalism. At the level of a multiple system it corresponds to the assumptions of consensus and commensurate requirements formulated at lower levels. Together these assumptions constitute the basic framework of this particular image of society, which Dahrendorf (1968) fondly has called utopian.

The assumption of disintegration may be encountered in modern functionalism, both in anthropology and in sociology. A good illustration of the empirical application of this assumption is provided by Geertz (1957). Discussing the relationship between social and cultural systems, he observed:

> Though separable only conceptually, culture and social structure will then be seen to be capable of a wide range of modes of integration with

one another, of which the simple isomorphic mode is but a limiting case—a case common only in societies which have been stable over such an extended time as to make possible a close adjustment between social and cultural aspects [p. 233].

He suggests replacing the assumption of integration with the more realistic assumption of disintegration. "Cultural structure and social structure are not mere reflexes of one another but independent, yet interdependent variables [p. 249]." And, he applies this assumption to the explanation of a concrete event, the disruption of a funeral ceremony: "the disruption of a funeral . . . may be traced to a single source: an incongruity between the cultural framework of meaning and the patterning of social interaction, and incongruity due to the persistence in an urban environment of a religious symbol system adjusted to peasant social structure [p. 249]."

Another example that emphasizes disintegration between the social subsystem and personality is found in Levy (1952). He points out that a specific goal orientation typical for industrial societies, namely "a rise in the stratification system through objective achievements in competition on a highly universalistic basis," is obviously functional for the social system, for it affords a large field from which the system may select individuals to fill the positions of the social structure; at the same time, however, this goal orientation is dysfunctional for individual personalities: "In the face of widespread motivation for upward social mobility based on competitive achievement, many of the strivings are bound to be frustrated in seeking their goals [p. 178]."

All that was said in favor of the assumption of conflict and contradictory requirements of the social system may be restated mutatis mutandis in the present context. It seems obvious that the assumption of subsystemic disintegration represents more adequately the complex, heterogeneous, and inconsistent character of modern society, and in this sense, it is more satisfactory.

The Conceptual Framework of
Functional–Subsystemic Analysis

To recapitulate the conclusions of my argument: There are two additional general assumptions and two pairs of alternative particular assumptions that make up the model of a multiple system. These assumptions are presupposed by functional–subsystemic analysis, the final type of functional analysis to be distinguished.

In the context of functional–subsystemic analysis, some new concepts, both basic and specific, appeared. Thus, the language of functional analysis was significantly enriched.

The language of functional–subsystemic analysis contains three *basic concepts:* SYSTEM$_5$, conceived as a set of interrelated systems (whether simple, teleological, functional, or purposive); SUBSYSTEM, conceived as a set of interrelated elements sufficiently distinct from the other elements of the system to be treated as a separate whole on the subordinate level; and FUNCTION$_5$, conceived as the contribution of the element to the maintenance or attainment of some preferred state(s) in the subsystems of the system to which it belongs.

Within the framework set by the general assumptions, a variety of particular solutions is possible. Their adoption introduces a series of *specific concepts* into the language of functional–subsystemic analysis. The most important are: *dysfunction$_3$, functional unity, functional disunity, subsystemic integration,* and *subsystemic disintegration.*

The problem of the empirical adequacy of the model of a multiple system, as well as of all the other systemic–functional models, is taken up in subsequent chapters.

PART III

THE GENERALIZED SYSTEMIC-FUNCTIONAL MODEL
Three Charges Refuted

Chapter 11

THE PROBLEM OF
EMPIRICAL ADEQUACY

Now that the systemic–functional models have been reconstructed, I must attempt to give them some justification. No conceptual model can be justified by intrinsic criteria alone. It is not enough for the model to be coherent, precisely defined, or perhaps esthetically rewarding. The model is conceived in instrumental terms as the tool of theory construction, and so the prime consideration in its appraisal must be given to extrinsic criteria, specifically, to its usefulness. Conceptual models receive their justification in the process of theory construction. They are valid only insofar as they generate testable and confirmed propositions or, to put it more precisely, insofar as the assertions formulated within the range of variability circumscribed by the model ultimately turn out to be verifiable and more important, are verified.

It may seem that the only manner of justifying a conceptual model is after the fact, when the model has already generated a theory, and when that theory has been subjected to rigorous assessment. If this were true, however, judgment would have to be suspended until the systemic–functional models had generated a full-fledged functional theory of society, and until that theory had survived empirical testing. At the outset, in other words, each model would appear equally adequate.

Fortunately there exist certain *prima facie criteria* which allow one, at least tentatively, to distinguish promising models from sterile ones. Namely, there is a particular condition which is necessary (though not sufficient) for the model to be useful in the sense specified earlier, and so the potential usefulness of the model may be appraised even before it is actually tested; at least an inadequate model may thus be rejected. Because the condition in question is a necessary, but not a sufficient, one, it certainly does not guarantee that the model satisfying it will be fruitful, but it does guarantee that the model which does not satisfy it will be sterile.

The condition I have in mind amounts to a *certain degree of fit* between the model and the domain of reality that the theory generated by the model is to explain. In order to be potentially useful the model must be to a certain extent *isomorphic* with the problematic domain of reality, or to put it otherwise, the problematic domain of reality must constitute an adequate empirical interpretation of the model. As Meadows (1957) commented:

> The formulation of a model consists in conceptually marking off a perceptual complex. . . . Every model is a pattern of symbols, rules and procedures regarded as matching, in part or in totality, an existing perceptual complex. Each model stipulates, thus, some correspondence with reality, some relevance of items in the model to the reality, and some verifiability between model and reality [p. 4].

With respect to systemic models, the same criterion was suggested by Lopreato (1971):

> Strictly speaking, we are justified in speaking of actual phenomena as "systems" in the proportion in which the ideal system is isomorphic with, or accurately encompasses, the phenomena it was constructed to represent. Needless to say, such justification decreases with the complexity of "the real world" and the proliferation of analytically relevant factors" [p. 310].

Thus, it is possible to justify a model partially, ex ante, by applying this criterion to it, without recourse to all theories that it generates or may possibly generate in the future. In the present part of this volume I shall attempt to answer the question of whether systemic–functional models, as reconstructed in Part II, are to some extent isomorphic with social reality and, consequently, whether prima facie evidence testifies in favor of their ultimate fruitfulness.

To be sure, a complete answer to this question would require a knowledge of social reality that we presently lack—precisely because of the scarcity of comprehensive well-substantiated theories. To appraise the degree of fit means to compare, and to compare means to know both things that are to be compared, in our case both the model and the reality it is supposed to represent. But there are some general assertions about social reality that we agree upon, as one may put it, over and across the borders of theoretical and methodological schools. The strategy of my appraisal consists of determining whether the systemic–functional models interpreted in the domain of social reality violate any of these fundamental assertions.

The traditional critique of systemic–functional models focuses on three assertions of this kind, which the models presumably violate: the *deterministic* character of social reality; the *dynamic* character of social reality; and the *historic* character of social reality. I shall call these criticisms charges of teleological, static, and ahistoric biases.

Each of the charges will be analyzed in terms of three questions. First, I shall ask in each case what is the real CONTENT of the charge, i.e., to what discrepancy between the interpreted model and the agreed upon properties of social reality does it specifically point. Second, I shall ask in each case what is the proper OBJECT of the charge, i.e., to which of the systemic–functional models, or more specifically, to which assumptions of the models does it refer. Third, I shall ask what is the FORCE of the charge, i.e., whether the deficiency it ascribes to systemic–functional models is a necessary, principal one, insurmountable within the assumptions of the model; or, is it a contingent, factual defect that relates to some particular applications or implementations of the models, but not to the models themselves, in which case it is surmountable without rejecting the models.

I shall attempt to prove that all three charges are unfounded with respect to *generalized systemic–functional models,* which of themselves do not violate either the axiom of determination, or that of dynamics, or that of historicity. As a result, in this crucial respect, systemic–functional models must be considered isomorphic with social reality. I shall consider my case sufficiently supported by giving a significant degree of plausability to the systemic–functional models—the degree that justifies basing further attempts at theory construction precisely on these models.

Chapter 12

THE CHARGE OF
TELEOLOGICAL BIAS

Explication of the Charge

Systemic–functional models are often spoken of as teleological. This attribution may be understood in two ways. First, it may be conceived as purely descriptive, emphasizing the significance of relations of the "means–end" type within these models. There is no doubt that "means–end" relations play an important role in systemic–functional models (in fact, all five concepts of function are construed in terms of this relation). Thus, in this sense systemic–functional models are obviously teleological. But, "teleological" has an evaluative connotation—and one with strongly negative overtones. This is the sense implicit in the charge of a teleological bias, and it will be examined in this chapter.

The charge of a teleological bias seems to stem from a certain intellectual unrest, which could well be voiced in the form of two questions. The first asks whether teleological notions inherent in systemic–functional models are not an unfortunate heritage of doctrinal teleology, so frequently encountered in ontological conceptions such as creationism, vitalism, or immanentism. The second asks whether the occurrence of teleological notions in systemic–functional models is not an indication of the penetration into the social sciences of commonsense, nonscientific ideas.

Both in their doctrinal and commonsense versions, teleological notions are based on at least one of two assumptions, each of which
blatantly contradicts the unquestionable, as it seems, axioms of present-day science. One is the assumption of extraempirical entities, final
principles which, themselves inexplicable, are supposed to explain
everything. Be it the transcendent metaphysics of God, the maker
and guide of the world, or the immanent metaphysics of pantheistic
Nature, entelechy, or élan vital, the *empiricist principle*—that only
those objects which are accessible to empirical, intersubjective cognition may be considered the subject matter of science—makes us treat
such and similar concepts as prescientific or even antiscientific. The
second assumption is that of a specific determination of present phenomena by future ones, i.e., those which, by definition, do not exist
at present. The *deterministic principle,* asserting that nothing can
emerge from nothing, or, in other terms, that only existing objects
can influence some other ones, leads us to reject finalistic conceptions.

Thus, to put it briefly, the charge of a teleological bias amounts
to the assertion that the interpretation of systemic–functional models
in the realm of social reality involves at least one of two assumptions
which seem totally unacceptable: the assumption of metaphysics, or
the assumption of finalism, or both.

Does this charge refer to all types of systemic–functional models
or only to some of them? This is equivalent to the question of which
assumptions of systemic–functional models can possibly have metaphysical or finalistic implications, as interpreted in a social context.
It seems obvious that the four assumptions of the simple-system model
are untainted in this respect. The assumptions of plurality, wholeness,
integration, and boundary cannot possibly suggest any notion of a
prime mover or final causes. The same is true of the assumptions
of the multiple-system model. Neither the assumption of the plurality
of systems, nor that of subsystemic heterogeneity, nor that of boundary
interchange have any metaphysical or finalistic flavor. But when we
come to the middle levels of our hierarchy of models, we encounter
some assumptions that easily lend themselves to this kind of interpretation. The relevant assumptions are: directive organization, self-regulation, double-level directive organization, double-level self-regulation,
purposeful rationality, integration of individual purposes, and systemic
goals.

What is common to all these assumptions is that some selected
state of affairs (be it a preferred state of the system as a whole,

or the functional requirements of the system, or the sociocentric purposes of an individual) is brought about automatically, by virtue of the fact that it belongs to a selected class of states; or, something comes about just because it should come about. The problem here is one of mechanism: How does it happen that preferred states of the system are sometimes achieved, that needs are sometimes satisfied, and purposes are sometimes realized.

The search for the *mechanism* may follow two paths. One is to adopt the external, *molar point of view* (or black-box approach). Then, the only way of describing the mechanism is to postulate a feedback between the final state of the system and its initial state, as well as all intermediate states in the chain of transformations. When the basic principle of this mechanism is examined a little more thoroughly, it appears that its use is quite limited in our context, and for several reasons. First of all, the final state of a system undergoing a teleological process is by definition later in time than the process itself, and of course, much later than the beginning of that process. Hence, if we assume the influence of that state on the earlier states, then, regardless of the terms used, we come up against the finalistic assumption in a new guise. Second, the final state may remain unattained for reasons of fact or of principle. A man running after a bus may miss it after all, and yet we shall not hesitate to explain his frantic efforts by that ultimately unattained goal. Moreover, the process may move toward a goal that cannot be reached at all. In both cases it would be a metaphysical absurdity to assume a determining influence, whether feedback or not, of something which does not, and sometimes even by definition cannot, exist (cf. Scheffler, 1958).

These difficulties lead us to seek a solution in a different direction. Thus, we abandon the molar, external approach and seek the mechanism of directive organization and self-regulation inside the system. We adopt the inner, *molecular point of view*. If we can assume that the system has a built-in mechanism that pushes it toward the preferred goal state in spite of changing circumstances, i.e., that it has a sort of inner program oriented to that final state, then we obtain a solution free from both metaphysical and finalistic overtones. But before we can accept such an assumption the mechanism in question must be precisely explicated, its anatomy must be described in scientific terms. In formal terms it has been successfully achieved. I have quoted some formal explications of this mechanism provided by Nagel,

Braithwaite, and Hempel. But the crucial problem now becomes whether at the moment of giving a substantive interpretation to systemic–functional models in the realm of social reality, one is not necessarily committed to some *auxiliary assumptions* of metaphysical or finalistic character. It is a quite reasonable supposition that, as Rudner (1966) put it: "If the transition is to be made from our example system to an actual one (if the skeleton is to be fleshed out) it will likely be necessary to add and incorporate many complicated hypotheses or laws into the theory of the actual system [p. 102]."

Let me try to interpret in a substantive, sociological context one of the assumptions of systemic–functional models which seems most vulnerable to the charge of teleological bias; namely, the assumption of self-regulation. The conclusions will apply mutatis mutandis to other problematic assumptions as well.

The assumption of self-regulation may be interpreted in two domains. The first, characteristic of all individualistic, psychologistic, and reductionistic trends in sociology, is the sphere of individual actions. The second, characteristic of all holistic and antireductionistic trends, is the sphere of social processes par excellence. I shall be mainly interested in the second domain, which is the proper realm for systemic–functional models, in the sense that they have been mainly constructed with this domain in mind. Yet, it seems heuristically advisable to start the analysis in the individualistic domain. By contrast, the problems that appear when systemic–functional models are applied to the social domain will be thrown into better relief.

What additional assumptions must be made if human behavior is seen as self-regulating? In this context the assumption of self-regulation would read as follows: If a given action is necessary or sufficient for the attainment of something, then this action will be taken up. Let us consider the two cases—the case of necessary conditions and the case of sufficient conditions—in turn.

The first auxiliary assumption qualifies the "something to be achieved" as an individual's goal, something that an individual wants. The second auxiliary assumption states that in the individual's belief a given action is necessary for the attainment of the goal. This belief need not be objectively true. The third auxiliary assumption pertains to the relation between the value of the goal and the costs of behavior (action), again in the subjective assessment of an acting individual. It states that in the individual's belief the value of the goal is greater than the costs of behavior necessary to attain the goal.

The assumption of self-regulation interpreted in the context of individual behavior appears to be nothing other than a *hypothesis of rationality* (in the subjective sense of the term) (cf. Hempel 1965: 463–473; Gibson 1960: 156–178). It can be phrased in the following way: If the individual strives for a certain goal and believes a certain action to be a necessary condition for attaining that goal, then, if the value of the goal is greater for the given individual than the costs of necessary action, the individual will take up this action.

When the assumption of self-regulation is understood in the sufficient-condition version, then one more auxiliary assumption is required in the process of interpretation. This is due to the fact that in this case a certain action is only one of the alternative possible actions, each of which bring about a given goal (at least in the assessment of the individual). The additional assumption states that for the individual the cost of a given action is less than the costs of any available alternative actions sufficient to attain his goal (to realize his purpose).

In this case the hypothesis of rationality has a somewhat more complicated form: If the individual strives for a certain goal and believes a certain action to be a sufficient, though not necessary, condition for attaining that goal, then, if the value of the goal is greater for the given individual than the costs of a selected action, and the cost of a selected action is smaller in his assessment than the cost of any possible alternative action that would lead to the same goal, then an individual will take up this action.

The empirical mechanism underlying the fitting of the appropriate action to the conceived goal is psychological in essence. It contains the conscious idea of the goal, as well as the means, and the choice of the best means to the goal, with subsequent modifications of behavior according to the perceived degree of attainment of the goal (cf. Ducasse 1949: 543–544; Scheffler 1958: 275–277). Thus, the interpretation of the assumption of self-regulation in the context of individual behavior seems well justified and does not imply any metaphysical or finalistic ideas.

The time has come to examine in a similar way the more difficult problems that are indicated by the semantic interpretation of the self-regulatory hypothesis in the context of social processes par excellence. What additional assumptions are required in this context? Are these assumptions acceptable?

The first auxiliary assumption qualifies the states to be achieved as preferred for the given system (either G states, N states, or P states). The second assumption states that a given element is necessary (or sufficient) for the attainment or maintenance of these states. The third assumption states that the objective value of the achievement of the preferred state is greater for the system than the cost of having the requisite element in the system. The fourth assumption, unavoidable in the sufficient-condition version of the second assumption, states that the objective cost of the given element is smaller for the system than the cost of alternative elements equally effective in bringing about the preferred state.

When these auxiliary assumptions are taken into account, the assumption of self-regulation receives the following interpretation: (*a*) if a certain state is preferred for a given system, and a certain element is a necessary condition for attainment or maintenance of that state, then, if the value of achieving the preferred state is greater for the system than the cost of a requisite element, the element will appear in the system; or (*b*) if a certain state is preferred for a given system, and a certain element is a sufficient condition for attainment or maintenance of that state, then, if the value of achieving the preferred state is greater for the system than the cost of a given element, and the cost of a given element is smaller for the system than the cost of alternative, equally effective elements, then the given element will appear in the system.

The similarity of the above formulation to the hypothesis of rationality is striking. But is this assumption equally legitimate in the context of social processes? There are several difficulties, but the most profound one has to do with the determination of the empirical mechanism responsible for the appearance of certain elements in the system if these elements are necessary conditions, or the most effective (say, cheapest) among sufficient alternative conditions of the system's preferred states. As Homans (1962) formulated it: "Suppose that a particular institution were good (functional) for a society. But what produced the fit between the institution and the good of that society [p. 27]?" The most precise determination of a system's preferred states or functional requirements will be valueless if one cannot point to the actual mechanism that achieves these states and fulfills these requirements. There are four ways in which functionalists approach this important issue.

The Evolutionary Mechanism

The first and most often encountered approach amounts to postulating some sort of evolutionary mechanism operating in the history of human society and based on the principle of random mutations, natural selection, and heredity. This is an obvious extension of the organic analogy, this time on the philogenetic level. In a much simplified form the typical argument would run like this: In the process of historical development some societies created a certain institution, say E, while others did not. It is irrelevant why this institution was created in the first place, it may be ascribed to blind accident or random mutation. In any case, the institution E proved of importance in the society's competition with other societies. Having positive survival value, it helped the society that possessed it to survive and to eliminate other societies that did not possess it. The same argument may be applied to any institution of society. As a result we supposedly observe a close correspondence between existing institutions and the preferred states or functional requirements of society. To put it briefly, those societies have persisted in which institutions conducive to persistence developed, while others have perished. Thus, in the long run the preferred states of the system or its functional requirements have been satisfied by the emergence of appropriate institutions.

Let me quote some examples of arguments of this type. Discussing the role of a common value system in the proper functioning of society, Davis (1949) wrote:

> We hold that the possession of common ultimate values by the members of different societies arose in the process of societal evolution. It resulted from the process of natural selection on a societal basis. In the struggle against nature and in the struggle between one human society and another, only these groups survived and perpetuated their culture which developed and held in common among their members a set of ultimate ends. Such possession (of common ultimate ends) is necessary for cohesion and group cooperation in any sociocultural system [p. 144].

And, similarly, Dore (1961) reconstructed some aspects of the Davis–Moore theory of stratification in the following manner:

> To take the example of stratification and the division of labor, the hypothesis would have to go something like this; for various reasons some societies which began the division of labor also had, or developed, a system of unequal privileges for different groups, others did not. Those which did functioned more efficiently as societies; perhaps they bred more rapidly than, acquired resources at the expense of, and eventually eliminated, the others. Perhaps . . . their obvious superiority

in wealth, power, the arts, standard of living etc., induced the others to imitate their institutions. . . . At any rate, by one, or a combination, of these processes it now happens that all societies with a division of labor have a system of stratification [p. 408].

Dore himself commented: "It is an unlikely story . . . [Dore 1961: 408]."

This comment reveals the doubts that are often expressed about the evolutionary mechanism in the social context. At least *four counterarguments* may be distinguished. The first contests the applicability of the principle of random mutations to the domain of social reality. The probabilistic logic of this principle demands practically infinite number of individual cases. The relatively short span of time covered by the history of human society, coupled with the relatively limited number of separate societies that existed in that time, precludes any precise use of the principle of random mutations, except in a figurative sense.

The second counterargument concerns the principle of natural selection and is well phrased by Homans (1962):

The competition between societies was something very different from the Darwinian struggle for existence. The weaker did not get eliminated, but in all but a few cases, absorbed. The victors were usually content to let the institutions of the weaker people alone so long as they themselves controlled the government and collected the taxes. It was impossible to demonstrate any general Darwinian mechanism that would eliminate dysfunctional institutions [p. 27].

The competition and conflict between human societies very rarely led to the complete annihilation of one of the parts, which is precisely the basic assumption of natural selection.

The third counterargument is directed against the principle of the hereditary fixation of adaptively (or, in our case, functionally) advantageous mutants in a societal context. This mechanism requires for its operation a very long time span. For reasons mentioned earlier, human society does not fulfill this necessary precondition.

The fourth counterargument raises some doubts as to the fundamental assumption that all evolutionary conceptions simply take for granted, namely, that there in fact is a close fit between social institutions and the preferred states or functional requirements of the social system. Harsanyi (1968: 307) aptly observes that even a superficial examination of social institutions reveals significant functional inefficiencies, and he directly rejects any assumption as to a perfect fit between what is and what should be. He adds that the constant attempts at social reform would be incomprehensible if this assumption held in human societies. Unfortunately, ours is not the best of all worlds, as some evolutionists would have us believe.

All these arguments are well taken, and in their light the evolutionary solution must be judged unsatisfactory, at least in its present form. But to dismiss this line of reasoning completely would be like throwing out the baby with the bath water. Perhaps the case is similar to that of the organic analogy. Taking a concrete case of evolution as an analogy for social evolution may be misleading for the same reasons as taking an organism for the model of society. Namely, it focuses attention on the specific properties of biological evolution and not on the general properties of evolution as such. But is it not at least conceivable to generalize the concept of evolution in a manner parallel to that applied to the concept of the organism? Probably Rapoport (1967) was correct that "there are even more general laws of evolution of which biological and linguistic evolutionary processes are special manifestations. . . . Studies of evolutions other than organic will enlarge this conceptual repertoire and will put already existing concepts into a more general context [p. 128]." Such a *generalized notion of evolution*, parallel to the generalized notion of system, could probably suggest the mechanism we are seeking. Although the task remains to be performed, its eventual completion seems to promise the solution of the teleological dilemma in functionalist thinking.

The Rational Mechanism

Some new ways of solving the problem of the mechanisms which bring into existence the elements necessary for the attainment or maintenance of the system's preferred states appear in the context of the purposeful-system model. Here the possibility exists that the "macroteleological" properties of the social system as a whole may be explained by the "microteleological" properties of individual human actions. The problem of motivations which make individuals act in a way functional to the preferred states of the system, or to put it otherwise, the problem of integration of individual purposes and system goals, is brought into the focus of analysis. What is the mechanism that translates social requirements into personal wishes? How does it come about that in many cases an individual attempting to realize his purposes contributes, by the same action, to social good?

The simplest answer posits a sort of rational mechanism. The argument, in simplified form, runs somewhat like this: The members of a society have a full and adequate knowledge of the social goals (global preferred states of the system or social requirements), as well as of the best means to achieve them, and they take this knowledge into account as the basic motivation behind their own actions. As a result, there is a complete integration of individual and social goals, of the egoistic strivings of people and the general good.

It seems obvious that the picture of an individual in society drawn here is fundamentally misleading. The assumed image of man is patently utopian, human actions are construed as perfectly rational (in the objective sense), and what is more, all human actions are seen as directed toward supraindividual ends. Homans (1962) captured the essential inadequacy of this image in the following words:

> We have no doubts that primitive men think rationally about their own societies. We do doubt that intelligent recognition that a certain institution would be good for a society is ever sufficient—though it may be a necessary—condition for its adoption. If it were, the history of human society would be happier than we observe it to be [p. 216].

If the rational mechanism is called forth to account for the actions or institutions functional for society, one encounters a new form of utilitarianism accompanied by all the philosophical doubts pertaining to this doctrine. And, conversely, if the rational mechanism is called forth to account for the actions or institutions dysfunctional in society, we are very close to the doctrine that Popper (1960) called "the conspirational theory of society" and characterized as searching at the root of all social troubles for somebody's wicked intentions and the antisocial actions of individuals or groups. Both these approaches seem obviously inadequate.

But granted all this, it must be admitted that in some limited cases the rational mechanism may in fact be operating. I have in mind the case of *rational social planning* based on the scientific diagnosis of the relevant situation, the delimitation of possible courses of action, the prediction of expected outcomes of each possible alternative action, and the choice of action based on explicit value priorities. The growing role of social, political, and economic planning enlarges the scope of situations in which individual actions or social institutions are effected precisely because they are supposed to serve some general consensual goal. In such cases the rational mechanism provides the missing link in the interpretation of systemic–functional models.

The Normative Mechanism

A different solution is given by authors emphasizing the normatively determined aspects of human action. According to the proponents of the normative mechanism, the integration of individual and social goals is brought about by the full internalization by the members of a society of that society's norms and values, and the consequent motivational importance of internalized norms and values in guiding individual actions. This type of mechanism is assumed by Bredemeier (1955:180), who in his catalogue of methodological rules for functional analysis included the postulate of searching for the normative criteria of gratification determining a given action. This approach is also very characteristic for Parsons (1951) and his school. Parsons is quite explicit on this point:

> The integration of a set of common value patterns with the internalized need–disposition structure of the constituent personalities is the core phenomenon of the dynamics of social systems. That the stability of any social system except the most evanescent interaction process is dependent on a degree of such integration may be said to be the fundamental dynamic theorem of sociology [p. 42].

Lockwood (1956), in his criticism of Parsons, brought this aspect of *The Social System* (Parsons 1951) to the fore: "Parsons' array of concepts is heavily weighted by assumptions and categories which relate to the role of normative elements in the social action, and especially to the processes whereby motives are structured normatively to ensure social stability [p. 284]." In another connection, he gives to Parsonian functionalism the name of "normative functionalism," which emphasizes its major theoretical focus.

Both in sociology and in social psychology there are numerous studies concerning the processes through which socially approved goals (values) become personal, private goals for the members of society, and socially approved means of attaining these goals (social norms) become the rules of individual conduct. On the macroscale these processes consist of socialization and social control. Parsons and Shils (1951) emphasized this very strongly: "The two main classes of mechanisms by which motivation is kept at the level and in the direction necessary for the continuing operation of the social system are the mechanisms of socialization and the mechanisms of social control [p. 227]." They go on to characterize these mechanisms in detail. On the microscale the processes of socialization and social control are seen as based on the psychological principles of learning, reward-seeking, deprivation avoidance, and the like. The appraisal of these theoretical ideas lies beyond the scope of this volume.

What seems most relevant in the present context is the question of the extent to which the normative mechanism provides the real missing link in the interpretation of systemic–functional models. For even if we grant that the processes of internalization of norms and values are represented adequately, or to put it differently, that we know the way in which social norms and values are transformed into individual rules and purposes, we still are left with the crucial problem of why these norms and values themselves are fitted to the preferred states of the system or to its functional requirements (assuming that there is a fit of this kind). What mechanism safeguards the correspondence between that which is "good" for the system, and that which the system requires of its members in the prescriptions and proscriptions of its normative structure? In short, the crucial matter of the *origins of social norms and values* remains without answer.

Thus, the solution provided by the normative mechanism seems apparent, rather than real, at least in its present form. It evades the problem through postulation: Why do individuals behave in sociocentric ways? The answer: Because they are led to do so by social norms and values. When the questions of why the norms are themselves sociocentric, why they are functional for the system's preferred states or functional requirements, are phrased, an appeal is usually made to one of the mechanisms discussed previously: In cases of "mores and folkways," to the evolutionary mechanism, and in the case of "laws," to the rational mechanism of legislation. In both instances one encounters the same problems and the same limitations that we have already discussed.

The Structural Mechanism

The last solution that is sometimes suggested may be called the structural mechanism. Here the integration of preferred states or functional requirements of the system and individual goals is considered the result of the direct influence of existing structural arrangements on the motivation of the individual acting within the framework of these arrangements. An example of an analysis utilizing this approach may be found in an essay by Homans and Schneider (in Homans 1962) on the forms of marriage in primitive society. That essay is explicitly conceived as a rebuttal to Levy-Strauss's theory explaining the spread of a particular form of marriage by its specific role in safeguarding social solidarity. Homans and Schneider argue that "to account for the adoption by a society of a particular institution, it is, in principle, never sufficient to show that the institution is in some sense good for the society, however that good may be defined [p. 214]." The "theory of a final cause" must always be supplemented by the "theory of an efficient cause." In the case of unilateral cross-cousin marriage, the theory of the requisite kind should: "(1) show the relation between different forms of unilateral cross-cousin marriage and other institutions, and (2) cite adequate individual motivation, aside from intellectual recognition that it is 'good' for a society, to account for the adoption of a particular marriage rule [Homans 1962: 217]." How do Homans and Schneider propose to construct such a theory?

According to the rule of unilateral cross-cousin marriages, a man is supposed to marry his mother's brother's daughter or his father's sister's daughter. In some societies the first form, matrilateral cross-cousin marriage, is the rule; in others, it is the patrilateral form. What factor can explain this variance? The hypothesis of Homans and Schneider claims that the choice of a marriage rule is dependent on the overall structure of society and, more directly, on the individual motivations shaped by this specific structure. The crucial aspect of social structure is defined as the locus of jural authority over ego, and the general hypothesis states that "the choice of form would be determined by the locus of jural authority over ego and the consequent pattern of interpersonal relations among kinsmen [p. 247]." This hypothesis, coupled with some common-sense psychological assumptions to the effect that "authority discourages intimacy [p. 248]" and that in order to marry someone the individual must be emotionally attached to him or her in the first place, supports the following argument: In patrilineal societies, in which jural authority over ego before marriage rests with the father, the individual is apt to direct his emotional allegiances toward his mother's kin, from whom he does not encounter dominance; consequently, he will typically marry his mother's brother's daughter. Conversely, in matrilineal societies, in which jural authority over ego rests with the mother's brother, the individual is apt to direct his emotional allegiance toward his father's kin; consequently, he will typically marry his father's sister's daughter. This provides an explanation for the predominance of matrilateral cross-cousin marriage in patrilinear societies, and patrilateral cross-cousin marriage in matrilinear societies.

Were this explanation valid and confirmed, it nevertheless would still raise some doubts and leaves some questions unanswered. Recall first that it was supposed to supplement Levi-Strauss's theory of final cause. (Levi–Strauss claims that matrilateral cross-cousin marriage is dominant in human societies because it contributes to "organic solidarity.") Homans and Schneider transfer the problem to a different level. They claim that the matrilateral cross-cousin marriage is dominant because most often the social structure has a patrilineal character, and the link between this type of structure and this type of marriage practice is provided by their theory. But why is this particular character of the social structure dominant? Levi-Strauss would answer, because it contributes to the "organic solidarity" of society. Homans and Schneider stop short of any answer. For them, the form of structure is a given, and further unexplainable premise.

We encounter in this example a difficulty very similar to that in the case of the normative mechanism. The answer is apparent, rather than real, insofar as it is supposed to furnish the linking mechanism determining that the institutions functional for society will automatically appear in that society. In order to explain the dominance of the patrilineal structure one would have to appeal again to evolutionary or rational conceptions—or, perhaps, devise another solution.

To recapitulate my argument: There exists an adequate *formal* explication of the mechanism of goal-seeking allowing one to conceive of the teleological properties of systems without any finalistic or metaphysical assumptions. As to the *substantive* interpretation of this mechanism in the domain of social reality, none of the solutions suggested in the literature can be considered as fully adequate and satisfactory.

All of them leave some questions without answers. But at least two of them, the evolutionary and rational solutions, seem to offer the possibility for refinement. If they are properly generalized and made precise, the missing link between the system's goals and the existence of social institutions or individual actions contributing to these goals will be provided. Or, perhaps, some other, better solution will be found. Anyway, there seems to be an opportunity to interpret the teleological properties of a social system without any appeal to metaphysical or finalistic ideas. The charge of a teleological bias, conceived as a necessary and insurmountable (and not only factual) defect of systemic–functional models, must be seen as rather unfounded.

Chapter 13

THE CHARGE OF
STATIC BIAS

Explication of the Charge

The most common criticism of functionalism has to do with its alleged static bias. One of the most vociferous critics of the functional school, Dahrendorf (1968), contends that "recent theoretical approaches [it is functionalism that he has specifically in mind], by analyzing social structure in terms of elements characteristic of immobile societies, have in fact assumed the utopian image of society [p. 112]." Referring to traditional functionalism, Homans (1971) remarked: "In the beginning the analyses tended to be static, as it is more convincing to speak of a social structure in a society conceived to be stable than in one undergoing rapid change [p. 103]." According to Buckley (1967), the Parsonian version of functionalism is characterized by "constant theoretical emphasis on the stable, equilibrating, harmonious aspects of society, he avoids systematic treatment of the conflicting, disequilibrating, disorganizing aspects of society that are not merely deviant and thus taken care of by his mechanisms of control [p. 184]." And Lockwood (1964) finds in "normative functionalism" some "unwarranted assumption that the study of social stability must precede the analysis of social change [p. 245]."

But even superficial reflection on the notion of stability as employed in these criticisms brings us to the conclusion that the charge is as common as it is ambiguous. One must attempt to explicate the charge in more precise terms before any judgment may be passed as to its validity.

What does it mean that an image of society invoked by this or that conceptual model is static? The first answer that comes to mind would read thus: Within the model it is impossible to conceptualize *social change* (any social change). But this is only an apparent solution. No orientation in modern social science raises any doubt as to the changing properties of social reality. It is everywhere considered an axiom (or perhaps a truism), irrespective of theoretical or methodological stances. It is also obviously accepted by functionalists. For this reason, the defense of functionalism against the charge of static bias understood in this general sense (by demonstrating that within systemic–functional models one may speak of change as such) misses the real point. One example of such a misdirected defense of functionalism is to be found in a paper by Cancian (1960), who indulges in very sophisticated argumentation to prove a claim that nobody doubted in the first place, namely that "there is no logical reason why a functional analysis cannot be useful in investigating change [p. 823]."

So the charge of a static bias must be construed in a more restricted way. If it does not challenge the ability of systemic–functional models to implement change per se, perhaps it challenges their ability to implement some *specific type of change*. Following this suggestion one may distinguish two types of social change, taking into account its genetic characteristics, i.e., a locus of the source, determinant, or initiating factor of change. In the first of the possible cases, the source of change cannot be described within the framework set by the assumptions of the model (in terms of its characteristic conceptual apparatus); hence, it must be considered as given and, further, inexplicable (anyway, short of constructing some other model, more comprehensive in this particular respect). All changes taking place in the model must be considered as some type of reaction to outside transformations of unspecified character. If there were no outside transformations, no environmental changes, the model itself would not change at all. This is the first case. In the second case, the source of change can be described within the assumptions of the model (in terms of its characteristic conceptual apparatus) and, therefore, it can be identified and accounted for. The model includes the preconditions of its own immanent transformations. With no regard for outside environmental changes, the model itself is constantly changing.

Change whose source lies outside the system's boundaries is usually called *exogenous change*. And change whose source lies inside the boundaries of a system is usually referred to as *endogenous change*. Applying this terminology we can say that in the first case the model is able only to conceptualize exogenous change and unable to conceptualize endogenous change, whereas in the second case the model is equally able to conceptualize both types of change. I suggest that the model of the first type be considered static, and the model of the second type as dynamic. When systemic–functional models are accused of a static bias, the content of the charge is best rendered by the following formulation: The models underlying functional analysis are inherently unable to conceptualize endogenous change.

Refutation of the Charge

Is this charge justified? And what is its force? I propose to show that the charge of a static bias applies only to some specific particular assumptions of systemic–functional models, and not to general assumptions. Consequently, the presumed static bias is not a *principal*, necessary, and insurmountable defect of functionalism as such, but at most a *factual* defect of some particular types of functionalism. To prove this point I propose the following strategy: If some of the particular assumptions appear conducive to the conceptualization of endogenous change, and some appear detrimental in this respect, then clearly the general assumptions that generated both types of particular ones must be regarded as totally free of the charge. If, within the same general framework one may construct both static and dynamic pictures, the framework should not be criticized if the picture happens to be static. The framework itself has obviously nothing to do with the static versus dynamic controversy.

It seems to me that the static or dynamic features of the model are determined by the choice of particular alternative assumptions along the 10 dimensions of structural variability generated by the general systemic–functional models.

First, the assumption of functional *reciprocity* has static implications, and the assumption of *exploitation*, dynamic ones. In the world of ideally equivalent, just, balanced, mutual exchanges there is no place for immanent change. But every case of unequivalent, exploitative exchange generates some type of conflict, strain, and, consequently, some potential for immanent transformations.

Second, the assumption of *consensus* has static implications, and the assumption of *conflict*, dynamic ones. Dahrendorf (1968) observed that "It is hard to see how a social system based on . . . universal consensus can allow for structurally generated conflicts. Presumably conflict always implies some kind of dissent or disagreement about values [pp. 115–116]." And, he adds: "By no feat of imagination, not even by the residual category of 'dysfunction' can the integrated and equilibrated social system be made to produce serious and patterned conflicts in its structure [p. 116]." What sources of change can be found in this peaceful world? Obviously only those lying outside, in the environment, but not inside the system. Only exogenous change is conceivable within such a framework. A quite opposite image is implied by the assumption of conflict. The recognition that contradictions, antagonisms, and conflicts constitute the fundamental features of social life, that "conflict can be temporarily suppressed, regulated, channeled and controlled, but that neither a philosopher–king nor modern dictator can abolish it once and for all [Dahrendorf 1968: 127]," points to the locus of dynamic tendencies. The endogenous change precipitated by intrasystemic, immanent sources is not only possible, but actually implied by this model.

Third, the assumption of *dependence* has static implications, and the assumption of functional *autonomy*, dynamic ones. If all the elements are totally dependent on the system and cannot possibly survive outside the system, then there is no conceivable stimulus for endogenous change. The vested interests of the elements will clearly refer to keeping the system intact, rather than changing it. The opposite consequences accompany the assumption of functional autonomy. Gouldner (1959) argued this point explicitly:

> Functional autonomy . . . focuses on the parts, albeit in their relations to each other; it directs attention to the possibility that any part may have little, as well as great, need for another, and that the mutual need of parts need not be symmetrical. In short, it focuses attention on interchanges where functional reciprocity may not be symmetrical, and thus directs analysis to tension-producing relationships. . . . The problem of functional autonomy is of considerable significance for the analysis of tension within social systems, and thus for the analysis of social change [p. 265].

The functional autonomy of elements leads directly to intrasystemic conflict. Let me trace some lines of Gouldner's argument. He assumes two opposite tendencies to operate within the social system. The first, which refers to the parts possessing some degree of functional autonomy, is the tendency to keep or even enlarge their scope of independence. The other, which refers to the system, is the tendency to limit the scope of the parts' independence, or even subordinate them to the system. These opposite tendencies produce intrasystemic strain. It may be expected that the elements that manage to acquire the largest scope of functional autonomy will become the foci of organized resistance against the integrating pressure of the system, and may become the potential generators of change. Defending its functional autonomy, an element may utilize several strategies. One of them is the strategy of "fight," i.e., the attempt to reorganize the system as a whole in order to safeguard its independent position. In this case, the objective "interest" of the element will call for the total transformation of the system. In effect, Gouldner (1959) suggests:

> What is a threat from the system's standpoint is a defensive maneuver from the part's standpoint. Conversely, the system's defenses against these are in turn, threats to the part's defenses. . . . In short, not only efforts to change the system, but also those directed at maintaining it are likely to entail conflict and resistance [p. 255].

Fourth, the assumption of *universal functionality* has static implications, and the assumption of dysfunction (or *specific functionality*), dynamic ones. There is no place for the source of change in a world in which all elements contribute harmoniously to the common cause. But if some elements are seen as "deviant" in this respect, they may justifiably be considered the loci of dynamic tendencies. And, if the number, or strategic importance, of "deviants" in the system exceeds those of positive contributors, change in the system seems inevitable. This point is made by Merton (1967): "The concept of dysfunction which implies the concept of strain, stress and tension on the structural level provides an analytic approach to the study of dynamics and change [p. 107]."

Fifth, the assumption of *uniform functionality* has static implications, and the assumption of *differential functionality*, dynamic ones. To be exact, endogenous change can also be conceptualized in the model comprising the first assumption, but the second assumption is much more satisfactory in this respect. The identification of elements (or classes of elements) exerting the strongest influence on the system's preferred states is tantamount to the identification of potential strategic sources of change. The eventual strain or conflict within the class of strategically important elements may be expected to bring about decisive changes in the system as a whole. The chances of effective changes being initiated among strategically important elements are much greater than the chances of changes stemming from the area of strategically less important elements.

Sixth, the assumption of *equilibrium* has static implications, and the assumption of *disequilibrium,* dynamic ones. This is almost self-evident. Within the model based on the principle of equilibrium (whether stable or unstable, static or moving), the conceptualization of endogenous change is precluded by definition. This point is made by Machlup (1958), who defined equilibrium "as a constellation of selected, interrelated variables so adjusted to one another that no inherent tendency to change prevails in the model which they constitute [p. 4]." All changes must be initiated outside the system, say, in the environment. The assumption of disequilibrium has exactly opposite ramifications. According to this assumption the actual structure of the system is constantly lagging behind the changing goal states of the system. There is a constant strain between the actual configuration of the elements in the system, and the configuration that would be functional for the actual preferred states of the system. There is also constant contradiction, antagonism, and conflict between the elements functional for the previous preferred state of the system (having "vested interests" in its petrification), and the elements potentially functional for the incoming state. All these strains, contradictions, antagonisms, and conflicts constitute the endogenous sources of systemic change.

Seventh, the assumption of *commensurate functional requirements* has static implications, and the assumption of *contradictory functional requirements,* dynamic ones. If the satisfaction of different functional requirements is mutually independent, i.e., is parallel, or even when it is positively correlated, then no strain can conceivably result in the process of need satisfaction. But when the satisfaction of one requirement stands in the way of satisfying another—when the processes "cross" at some point—then internal strain is immediately generalized in the system. This implication of the assumption of contradictory functional requirements was recognized clearly by Sjoberg (1967), who considered it as a "modification of existing structural–functional theory that will enable it better to incorporate sociological findings with respect to both social change and the recurrent tensions within and among social systems [p. 339]." The inclusion of this assumption in the conceptual model enables one to see the ways in which "the antagonisms among these varied imperatives can induce either tension or outright conflict that may eventually initiate social change [Sjoberg 1967: 340]." Two analytically distinct situations seem possible: First, some different elements functional for various mutually contradictory requirements will be objectively contradictory—this may lead to antagonisms or conflicts between them; second, one and the same element simultaneously serving two contradictory requirements will develop contradictions which may lead to powerful internal strains. In both cases there are significant changes of systemic change.

Eighth, the assumption of *constant requirements* has static implications, and the assumption of *changing requirements,* dynamic ones. If the functional requirements of the system are constant, then there is no reason for the given set of structural arrangements to undergo change. Once such structural arrangements are established, there is a tendency to maintain the status quo. But, if the requirements themselves change, then the actual structural arrangements will always be unsatisfactory; they will always be lagging a step behind the changing needs. In order to satisfy new needs, the structure must be modified. The system experiences a constant internal strain, as well as antagonisms and conflicts between the elements functional for the old needs and elements functional for the new needs. This creates an important intrasystemic source of change.

Ninth, the assumption of *functional unity* has static implications, and the assumption of *disunity,* dynamic ones. If the functions of the element with respect to different subsystems are the same or mutually congruent, there is no conceivable source of strain. But if the opposite situation obtains, and a given element serves divergent functions for different subsystems, being functional for some and dysfunctional for others, then strains, contradictions, antagonisms, and conflicts immediately result. This in turn may lead to structural change in the system. Radcliffe-Brown (1952) recognized this possibility quite clearly when he introduced the notion of *dysnomia,* as opposed to *eunomia,* or functional unity: "A society that is thrown into a condition of functional disunity or inconsistency (for this we now provisionally identify with dysnomia) will not die . . . but will continue to struggle toward some sort of eunomia, some kind of social health, and may, in the course of this, change its structural type [p. 183]."

Tenth, the assumption of *subsystemic integration* has static implications, and the assumption of *subsystemic disintegration,* dynamic ones. If the subsystems are mutually congruent and harmonious, then strain, contradiction, and conflict are precluded by definition. But if the preferred states of several subsystems, or their functional requirements are mutually incompatible, then strains, contradictions, and conflicts are easily conceivable. Geertz (1957) has suggested:

> A revision of the concepts of functional theory so as to make them capable of dealing more effectively with "historical materials" might well begin with an attempt to distinguish analytically between the cultural and social aspects of human life and to treat them as independently variable, yet mutually interdependent factors. . . . In most societies where change is a charateristic rather than an abnormal occurrence, we shall expect to find more or less radical discontinuities between the two. I would argue that it is in these very discontinuities that we shall find some of the primary driving forces of change [p. 233].

To recapitulate, we have seen that within each pair of alternative particular assumptions, the acceptance of one extreme solution has static implications, whereas the acceptance of the other extreme alternative has dynamic implications. One may analytically construct a *static systemic–functional model* by combining general assumptions with the following set of particular assumptions: functional reciprocity, consensus, dependence, universal functionality, uniform functionality, equilibrium, commensurate functional requirements, constant functional requirements, functional unity, and subsystemic integration. And one may as well analytically construct a *dynamic systemic–functional model* by combining the general assumptions with the opposite set of particular assumptions: exploitation, conflict, autonomy, disfunction (or specific functionality), differential functionality, disequilibrium, contradictory functional requirements, changing functional requirements, functional disunity, and subsystemic disintegration.

If in the common framework of general assumptions it is equally possible to construct a static particular model as it is a dynamic particular model, then the framework itself is obviously neither static nor dynamic. Or to put it otherwise, if the general assumptions allow equally well for static particular assumptions and dynamic particular assumptions, then they are themselves neutral with respect to a static (or for that matter dynamic) bias. The static bias must not be considered as a principal and insurmountable deficiency of systemic–functional models as such, but, at most, as the factual defect of some particular implementations of these models.

There is hardly any doubt that traditional functionalism was heavily bent toward a static alternative. There were several factors that contributed to that bias. From a methodological point of view there is one factor especially that requires comment. As I have mentioned earlier, the inspiration of functionalism originated in biology. In transferring the organic model of biological science to anthropology and sociology, the early functionalists ascribed to society not only the general properties of an organism whereby it exemplifies a system, but also the particular properties which make it an example of a static system. Thus, the uncritical application of the organic analogy seems primarily responsible for the static bias of functionalism. Once again an old truth is confirmed: "A model may be a potential intellectual trap as well as an invaluable intellectual tool [Nagel 1961: 115]."

Insofar as functional analysis focused on isolated, primitive communities, the analogy worked quite well, and the model appeared useful, despite its bias. But this success was due to the accidental features of this specific type of society, and not to the fundamental properties of a social system as such. When sociological functionalism turned to the analysis of complex contemporary societies, the inadequacy of the static model was immediately brought into sharp relief. And, as a result, the dynamic functional model had to be developed. It is certainly far from complete, but I have tried to show that its development is well advanced.

Chapter 14

THE CHARGE OF
AHISTORIC BIAS

Explication of the Charge

Another very common criticism of functionalism has to do with its alleged ahistoric bias. Sometimes this criticism is lumped with the charge of a static bias. But I propose to distinguish both of them and to consider the charge of ahistoricism separately. Just as in the previous case, this charge must be precisely explicated before its force can be judged.

What does it mean that an image of society called forth by this or that conceptual model is ahistoric? It seems, again, that the charge has something to do with the ability of the model to incorporate *change*—but not any kind of change, only some specific type. I propose to distinguish types of change according to the criterion of its structural characteristics. What is the form of the process of change? What it is that changes in the process (what is the object of transformations)?

First, we may distinguish directive and nondirective social change, whereby *directive change* is understood as a series of interlinked transformations of some object in the course of which the state of the object comes ever closer to some standard state, and by *nondirective social change,* we understand singular, accidental, or cyclical transformations of the object. In the case where the standard state being achieved asymptotically by the process of change is evaluated positively in terms of some scale of values, we shall speak of *progress,* and when it is evaluated negatively, of *regress* (of course, from the point of view of that particular scale of values).

Second, we may distinguish *total change,* i.e., change *of* the system as a whole, and *partial change,* i.e., change *in* the system without the transformation of its overall identity. In the first case, all the elements of the system, the structure of their interrelations, its preferred states, and its functional requirements undergo some transformations, so that in principle a new system is created. In the second case, only some elements, relations, or states undergo transformations; so, the system retains its basic identity. Naturally there is a continuum, rather than dichotomy in question here, and in some intermediate instances the qualification of change according to this criterion may raise some difficulties. In sociology the criterion used most often refers to the "core institutional order" of society. If that order is transformed, the change is classified as total, and if that order is basically kept intact, despite some modifications, the change is classified as partial. These definitions may help to make precise the notion of development. Hence, by *development* I shall mean the process of directive and total change.

According to my reconstruction, the charge of an ahistoric bias means that within the framework of systemic–functional models, it is impossible to conceptualize the process of development in the sense just specified. As a result, the picture of society is not well specified in time and space. This meaning of ahistoricism is emphasized by Dahrendorf (1968), who finds it explicit in all utopian images of society: "All utopias from Plato's Republic to George Orwell's brave new world of 1984 have one element in common: they are all societies from which change is absent. . . . The social fabric of utopias does not, and perhaps cannot, recognize the unending flow of historical process [p. 107]." In such images, society has no past and no future; it is not conceived as a link in the historical chain of events, but rather as some absolute, unique entity. In Dahrendorf's view, the functionalist image of society shares this basic defect of all utopias.

But this reconstruction of the charge of ahistoricism tells only half the story. The second half has to do with the determination or modification of intrasystemic phenomena by the system's specific historical situation, i.e., by the very fact that it is only a link in the developmental chain. As such, it is codetermined, or modified, by three sets of circumstances: first, by the actual *historical context*—the wide array of phenomena making up its actual environment; second, by the *historical past*—the previous phases of its development which left some mark on its elements, relations, or states; and third, by the *expected or planned future*—the present vision of future states of the system. The reference of intrasystemic phenomena to the *historical situation* of the system in all three aspects we have distinguished may be called *historical relativization,* and the analysis which takes into account both the historical context, historical past, and historical perspectives of the system in question may be referred to as the concrete historical approach.

Thus, the second aspect of the charge of ahistoricism refers to the alleged inability of systemic–functional models to take into account the historical relativization of intrasystemic phenomena and processes, and consequently to lend itself to the concrete historical approach. It is claimed that within systemic–functional models, the conceptualization of the historical context, historical past, and historical perspectives is basically impossible.

To sum up, when systemic–functional models are accused of an ahistoric bias, the content of the charge is best rendered by the following formulation: Models of this type are inherently unable to conceptualize developmental change, as well as the modifying influence of the historical situation of the system as a whole, on the course of intrasystemic phenomena.

Refutation of the Charge

Is this charge justified? And, what is its force? I propose to show that the charge of ahistoric bias applies only to some particular assumptions of systemic–functional models, and not to the general assumptions. Consequently, the presumed ahistoric bias is not a *principal*, necessary, and insurmountable defect of functionalism as such, but only a *factual* deficiency of some particular types of functionalism.

To prove this point I propose to use the same strategy that was applied in the defense of functionalism against the charge of a static bias. Namely, I shall attempt to show that some of the particular assumptions have ahistoric implications, but some have historic ones, and as both are equally incorporated within the general framework of systemic–functional models, the models themselves are neither historic nor ahistoric. Hence, they are undeserving of the criticism. It seems to me that the ahistoric, or conversely historic, features of systemic–functional models are determined by the choice of particular alternative assumptions along the six dimensions of structural variability generated by the systemic–functional models.

First, the assumption of *isolation* has ahistoric implications; the assumption of *structural context* has historic ones. Obviously, the model which construes a system as totally isolated from the environment cannot take into account the historical situation of the system, which, in all three aspects, refers to environmental, extrasystemic phenomena, present, past, and future. But, by the same token, the opposite assumption that construes a system as significantly influenced by its environment is able to incorporate historical relativization.

Second, the assumption of *universal functionality* has ahistoric implications, and the assumption of *dysfunctions,* historic ones. The picture of a system in which all elements are functional for the whole excludes from consideration both the elements that were functional in the past, but no longer fulfill the same function (functional survivals), and the elements that still do not fulfill a given function, but will fulfill it in the future (functional "germs"). Both types of elements can be incorporated in the model when the opposite assumption is adopted. They may be considered as dysfunctional for the present state of the system, or neutral in this respect, depending on the nature of the concrete case. Besides, the model acquires the ability to handle a significant type of change which consists of the transformations of functional significance of a given element—from functionality to neutrality or dysfunctionality, and so forth in all possible combinations.

Third, the assumption of *equilibrium* has ahistoric implications, and the assumption of *disequilibrium,* historic ones. Within the model which assumes the unchanging, constant character of a system's preferred states, the only conceivable changes have a partial character; they are at most changes *in* the system (and not *of* the system), i.e., compensatory reactions to extrasystemic transformations restoring a disturbed or endangered equilibrium. If, on the other hand, one assumes the regular transformation of a system's preferred states, the model is able to conceptualize total change, the change of the system (and not only in the system) in all its relevant respects (new elements, new relationships, new preferred states).

Fourth, the assumption of *constant requirements* has ahistoric implications, and the assumption of *changing requirements,* historic ones. The reasoning behind this claim follows the same path as that in the previous case and does not need to be repeated.

In summary, we have seen that within each pair of selected alternative assumptions, the adoption of one extreme alternative has ahistoric implications and the adoption of the other extreme alternative, conversely, has historic implications. One may analytically construct an *ahistoric systemic–functional model* by combining the general assumptions with the following set of particular assumptions: isolation, universal functionality, equilibrium, and constant requirements. And, conversely, one may analytically construct a *historic systemic–functional model* by combining the general assumptions with the opposite set of particular assumptions: structural context, dysfunction (or specific functionality), disequilibrium, and changing requirements.

If, in the common framework of general assumptions it is equally possible to construct an ahistoric particular model and a historic particular model, then the framework itself is obviously neither ahistoric nor historic. Or, to put it otherwise, if the general assumptions allow equally well for ahistoric particular assumptions and historic particular assumptions, then they are themselves totally neutral with respect to an ahistoric bias. The ahistoric bias must not be considered a principal and insurmountable deficiency of functional–systemic models as such, but at most, as the factual defect of some particular implementations of these models.

There is no doubt that traditional functionalism was heavily bent toward ahistoricism. One of the circumstances that contributed to this initial ahistoric bias has to do with the type of data that were at the disposal of functionalists in anthropological field studies. There were no reliable historical records concerning the past of the communities studied, which as a rule were preliterate. And naturally, there were also no clear-cut visions of the future in the social consciousness of the primitives that could be taken into account as modifying present structural arrangements. The solution to this research situation was to construe the society in ahistoric terms. But it was purely accidental, and not necessarily implied by the functional perspective. One may point out that Malinowski himself did not refrain from constructing a historical picture of some African societies when he got hold of reliable historical sources.

The ahistoric image of society appeared totally inadequate with respect to modern, complex societies with written records and a well-developed historical consciousness—societies rich in historical sources of all kinds. As a result of changed research opportunities, sociological functionalism has moved slowly toward a historic frame of reference. The transition is certainly not completed yet. But the charge of ahistoricism, even in its weaker factual form loses more and more ground with respect to modern functionalism.

Chapter 15

SYSTEMIC–FUNCTIONAL MODELS IN THE MARXIST THEORY OF SOCIETY

Introduction

I want to close my defense of functionalism with the following argument: (*a*) without doubt, the orientation of contemporary sociology which is most consistently dynamic and historical in the sense specified in Chapters 13 and 14 is the Marxist theory of society; (*b*) if the functional orientation were static and ahistorical, then the assumptions of the conceptual models characteristic of functionalism would be contradictory to the assumptions of the conceptual models characteristic of Marxism; but (*c*) the assumptions of the conceptual models characteristic of Marxism are the same as the assumptions of the conceptual models characteristic of functionalism, though they are not explicit in Marxist works; (*d*) therefore, the functional orientation is neither static nor ahistorical.

The point to be proved is of course the third. The remaining points are either trivial or follow from the third by virtue of simplest logic. The discussion of the third point involves of necessity a limited comparison of the functional with the Marxist orientation.

Such a comparison may be conducted at three levels. First, one may examine the *genetic dimension* of comparison. Is Marxism an intellectual source that inspired functionalism? Or, do they originate from the same—a third—source? Or, are their origins independent? This is but a sample of questions relevant at this level. To answer them is the proper task for the historian of ideas. Second, one may examine the *pragmatic dimension* of comparison. What are the practical, political, or ideological consequences of adopting each of the approaches? Do they lead to similar or different suggestions for social engineering? Are their implications conservative, revolutionary, or perhaps neutral in this respect? Are they utilized as justifications for common or opposite causes? These kinds of questions can be answered in political philosophy and, perhaps, in political sociology. Yet, the answers, if forthcoming, would be irrelevant in the present context; thus, I will not address these questions. Third, one may examine the *analytic dimension* of comparison. Setting aside the matter of sources and consequences—where do they come from, and where do they lead to—one may inquire simply what is the content of both orientations.

Clearly, the problem involved in the third premise of my argument is to be solved on this analytic plane. I want to emphasize that I am not evaluating types of comparative study, I am only selecting one for my purposes. If one attempted a total confrontation of Marxism and functionalism, all three dimensions of comparison would have to be taken into account. But, for the limited comparative purpose I set myself in this chapter, only the analytic dimension is directly relevant.

It is not the only delimitation of my present discussion. The second has to do with the specific aspect of the extremely rich and heterogeneous content of both orientations that will be examined. Namely, I will be concerned only with their respective notions of society: What properties, both general and particular, do they ascribe to the domain of social reality; or, to put it otherwise, what are the conceptual models of society, both general and particular, that are assumed by them, whether explicitly or implicitly. I want to emphasize that my conclusions will be as limited as the question. Anybody who attempted a total confrontation of Marxism and functionalism at the analytic level would have to deal with their empirical hypotheses or assertions, as well as with their methodological prescriptions concerning the ways in which such assertions are to be generated. For the sake of my argument, the focus on the conceptual models assumed by both orientations is sufficient.

To state my case briefly: I claim that there is a *fundamental affinity* between Marxism and functionalism, based on the common conceptual models—systemic–functional models of society—assumed by both orientations. This affinity is limited to the general assumptions of the systemic–functional models; within the same frame of reference both orientations tend to make opposite choices as to the particular assumptions. They define in opposite ways the concrete values of social variables within the range of variability permitted by the model. Marxism tends to choose "dynamic" and "historic" assumptions, whereas functionalism (at least in its traditional forms) tends to choose "static" and "ahistoric" assumptions. But the frame of reference is the same, and it is enough to prove this point in order to refute once and for all the charge of the basic, insurmountable bias of the functional orientation as such.

The general assumptions making up the functionalist notion of society were discussed in Chapters 6, 7, 8, 9, and 10. Thirteen assumptions of this sort were distinguished. Let us see if the same assumptions may be reconstructed out of the Marxist notion of society.

Marx (1956) was often explicit as to the *analytic point of view* he takes in the study of society in general, as opposed to the study of historical examples of societies: "The relations of production in their totality constitute what is called the social reality, society . . . [p. 147]." In a different context: "The aggregate of the relations in which the agents of this production stand to Nature and to each other, and within which they produce, is precisely society [p. 155]." On this *analytic level* the Marxist notion of society is best expressed in his "theory of socioeconomic formation," whereas on the corresponding *concrete level*, the theories of classes, class conflict, collective interests, revolutionary struggle, etc., would obviously be relevant.

The foundations of Marx's theory of socioeconomic formation, developed most extensively in *Das Kapital*, are laid down in this famous passage from "The Preface to a Contribution to the Critique of Political Economy":

> In the social production of their life, men enter into definite relations that are indispensable and independent of their will, relations of production which correspond to a definite stage of development of their material productive forces. The sum total of these relations of production constitutes the economic structure of society, the real foundation on which rises a legal and political superstructure and to which correspond definite forms of social consciousness. . . . At a certain stage of their development, the material productive forces of society come into conflict with the existing relations of production. . . . From forms of develop-

ment of productive forces these relations turn into their fetters. Then begins the epoch of social revolution. With the change of economic foundation the whole immense superstructure is more or less rapidly transformed [1968: 182–183].

The *analytic model of society* implicit in the preceding remarks, as well as in several other statements by Marx, may be reconstructed by means of the following simple scheme:

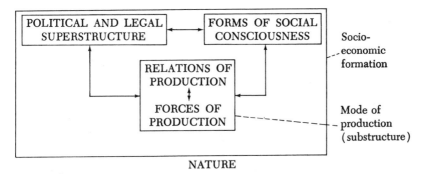

NATURE

(extrasocial environment + human hereditary endowment)

This is clearly a systemic–functional model of society. To support this claim, let me discuss the theory of socioeconomic formation in terms of the 13 assumptions of systemic–functional models that were defined.

The Assumption of Plurality

Society is obviously conceived as a plurality of heterogeneous elements. It includes technological equipment, human skills, relations of ownership, structures of power, superordination and subordination, patterns of production, distribution and consumption, political institutions, legal norms, ethical, esthetic, and religious ideas, ideologies, etc.

The Assumptions of Wholeness and of Integration

This set of elements is linked together by mutual, "dialectical" interrelations. Referring to a particular subset of social elements Marx observed: "The result at which we arrive is not that production, distribution, exchange and consumption are identical, but that they are the elements of a totality, distinctions within a unity. . . . There is interaction between the various elements. This is the case in every organic whole [1956: 18]." The organic like integration of social reality was also emphasized by Lenin (1949): "Society is not a simple, mechanical aggregate of these or those institutions, the simple, mechanical accumulation of these or those phenomena [p. 191]. . . . It is rather a social organism, holistic system of social relations, the social formation [p. 192]."

The Assumption of Boundary

There is a boundary between the socioeconomic formation and the environment. The concept of environment is implicit in the following statement by Marx:

> The first premise of all human history is, of course, the existence of living human individuals. The first fact to be established, therefore, is the physical constitution of these individuals and their consequent relation to the rest of nature. Of course we cannot here investigate the actual physical nature of man or the natural conditions in which man finds himself—geological, oro-hydrographical, climatic and so on [1956: 53].

Thus, the environment of the social system consists basically of extrasocial factors, as well as the hereditary endowment of its members. These factors influence society and are in turn influenced by society. As Marx (1956) put it: "Circumstances make men just as much as men make circumstances [1956: 55]."

The Assumption of Directive Organization

The series of transformations that the socioeconomic formation undergoes in time is defined as the historical process. The essence of the Marxist conception of the historical process is the acknowledgment of its orderly and directive character (described by the "laws of social development"). History is not an array of accidents, but a lawful series leading from the lower to the higher forms of social life. As Marx wrote: "In broad outlines Asiatic, ancient, feudal and modern bourgeois modes of production can be designated as progressive epochs in the economic formation of society [1968: 191]." This idea is well explained by Lenin: "The chaos and arbitrariness that had previously reigned in views on history and politics, were replaced by a strikingly integral and harmonious scientific theory, which shows how in consequence of the growth of productive forces, out of one system of social life another and higher system develops [1968: 24]." Among the types of socioeconomic formation, i.e., among the phases in the sequence of the historical process, each one has a particular character, yet all historical transformations are directed, in the long run, toward attainment of a selected phase. Its attainment ends "the prehistory of human society." This selected, or in our terms "preferred," state of the system is the classless, nonantagonistic socioeconomic formation. As Aron (1968) correctly observed, "For Marx the nonantagonistic, postcapitalist regime is not merely one social type among other; it is the goal, so to speak, of mankind's search for itself [p. 178]."

The Assumption of Self-Regulation

The orderly and directive mode of development of socioeconomic formation is brought about by particular internal mechanisms. The basic parts of society—the productive forces, the relations of production, and the legal and political superstructure—are interlinked by necessary lawful relations. These are sometimes called in the Marxist idiom, "the laws of necessary correspondence" (cf. Lange 1962) and designate the main feedback loops built into the system. By virtue of their operation, the initial change in the productive forces (brought about by the strains resulting from man's continual struggle with the natural environment) leads, by a series of compensatory changes in the structure of productive relations and in turn in the structure of legal and political institutions, toward the total transformation of the whole system, and the rise of a new socioeconomic formation. In modern terms this aspect of Marxist through is interpreted clearly by Afanasyev (1968):

> Marx and Engels created the science of society as a holistic, self-regulating system. . . . The socio-economic formation constituting a whole,

the totality of organically interrelated processes and events represents at the same time the dynamic and self-regulating system. Its functioning and development is not determined by some a priori goals, or supernatural forces, but by internal mechanisms, the factors of regulation. Thanks to the regulating mechanisms the social system can keep its identity as a whole, its state of dynamic equilibrium [p. 41].

The Assumption of Double-Level Directive Organization

In order for the socioeconomic formation to exist, some requirements must be met. Marx did not develop the catalogue of functional requirements in any systematic manner, but the idea itself was by no means alien to his thought. Particularly, he focused attention on the necessities created by the biological nature of man:

We must begin by stating the first presupposition of all human existence, and therefore all history, namely that men must be in a position to live in order to be able to make history. But life involves before anything else eating and drinking, a habitation, clothing and many other things. The first historical act is therefore the production of material life itself. This is indeed a historical act, a fundamental condition of all history, which today, as thousands of years ago must be accomplished every day and every hour merely in order to sustain human life [1956: 60].

Thus, the basic functional requirement of the social system is the production of goods. This is a universal requirement, common to all socioeconomic formations. But there are also historical requirements characteristic of particular types of socioeconomic formations. For example, in the capitalist formation such requirements include, in Marx's view, the accumulation of capital, the existence of the market, the transformation of labor into commodities, the average rate of profit, the existence of a "reserve industrial army," i.e., a certain amount of unemployment, etc.

The Assumption of Double-Level Self-Regulation

There are several mechanisms built into the socioeconomic formation that provide for the gradually improving satisfaction of its functional requirements in the course of historical development. The universal requirement of growing production and, consequently, better satisfaction of material needs, is met more and more adequately through progressive transformations of the mode of production by means of social revolutions. The particular requirements of a specific mode of production are also met by intrasystemic mechanisms. For example, the mechanism of competition between the different sectors of a capitalist economy provides for the establishment of the average rate of profit. If there were great disparities between the rates of profit in various sectors of the economy, the system could not function because of the lack of investment in the less profitable, but functionally necessary, branches. According to Marx, this explains why the rate of profit is not directly proportional to the surplus value.

The Assumptions of Purposeful Rationality and of the Integration of Systemic Goals with Individual Purposes

In Marx's view each member of society acting in his own interest contributes by the same action to the functioning, and to the eventual transformation, of the system as a whole. Marx claimed: "History is nothing but the activity of men aiming at their goals [1961: 114]." Engels elaborated this point: "In the history of society . . . the actors are all endowed with consciousness, they are men acting with deliberation or passion, working towards definite goals; nothing happens without conscious purpose, without an intended aim [1968: 622]." This is not equivalent to an individualistic approach nor to a voluntaristic approach. To claim, in Gellner's (1969) phrase, that all history is "about chaps" is not equivalent to constructing historical explanations "in terms of chaps [p. 268]." And, as Addis (1969) aptly pointed out: "To say that the course of history depends on what we will is not to say that history is as we will it [p. 335]." Marx was quite explicit on this point: "Mankind always sets itself only such tasks as it can solve, since . . . it will always be found that the task arises only when the material conditions of its solution already exist or are at least in the process of formation [1968: 183]." And, in a different connection, he argued the case even more emphatically: "Men make their own history, but they do not make it just as they please; they do not make it under circumstances chosen by themselves, but under circumstances directly encountered, given and transmitted from the past [p. 97]."

The Assumptions of Plurality and the Heterogeneity of Subsystems

Marx conceives of a socioeconomic formation as a complex and heterogeneous system made up of multiple subsystems. The basic subsystem, the "real foundation" supporting all the other components of society, is called the mode of production. It consists of productive forces together with the corresponding relations of production. In modern terms it is akin to an economic subsystem. The second subsystem is called the political and legal superstructure. It consists of political institutions and legal rules insofar as they serve the given mode of production, petrifying its characteristic structure of productive relations (and particularly the ownership of productive means). In modern terms it is akin to a political subsystem. And the third subsystem is described as the forms of social consciousness. It consists of ideas, values, and norms, which are inherent in the ethical, esthetic, religious, and artistic creations of the given epoch. In modern terms it is akin to a cultural subsystem (with the exception of civilizational or technological aspects which, for Marx, are included in the notion of productive forces).

The Assumption of Boundary Interchange

All three subsystems are mutually interrelated. Ultimately it is the mode of production which exerts a decisive influence on the character of the whole system, but the relationships are always double-sided. As Engels explained it in a famous letter to Bloch:

> According to the materialistic conception of history, the ultimately determining element in history is the production and reproduction of real life. More than this neither Marx nor I have ever asserted. Hence if somebody twists it into saying that the economic element is the only determining one, he transforms that proposition into a meaningless, abstract, senseless phrase. The economic situation is the basis, but the various elements of the superstructure . . . also exercise their influence upon the course of historical struggle and in many cases preponderate in determining their form [1968: 692].

Marxism and the Systemic Approach

I have attempted to demonstrate that the assumptions of systemic–functional models find their more or less explicit implementation in the Marxist image of society. The preceding discussion concerned the *general assumptions*. If one carried out a similar analysis of the *particular assumptions* adopted by Marx within the range of variability permitted by the general model, it would appear that as a rule his choices were opposite to those made by traditional functionalists. But, these choices are made *within the same general framework*—the framework of systemic–functional models. For my argument in this chapter, this conclusion is sufficient. If Marx could construct his dynamic and historical theory of society within the systemic–functional framework, then the framework itself cannot be considered as static and ahistorical.

If my analysis is valid, Marx may be pronounced the forefather of the modern systems approach in social science. The recognition of this aspect of Marxist thought is relatively recent. Only in the last decade have the problems of systems analysis become central to Marxist sociology in Eastern Europe and in the Soviet Union. Very fruitful results were reached in this respect in Poland by Lange (1962), Topolski (1968a,b, 1970), and the philosophical "school" centered at the University of Poznan. The major effort consists of applying the modern conceptual tools of philosophy of science, cybernetics, and related disciplines for the explication and creative examination of Marxist sociological ideas. Similar efforts are carried on in the Soviet Union (see Afanasyev 1968; Sadovsky 1966; Gershikov 1970; Blauberg and Yudin 1970), as well as in Czechoslovakia (Charvat 1970).

All these developments have had twofold results. First, they have brought about fundamental *changes in the conceptual apparatus* of theoretical sociological research; the concepts of system, structure, function, relationship, interaction, organization, etc., acquired a central place in the language of Marxist sociology. Second, the *strategy of research and theory construction* has changed accordingly. The codification of the methodological principles of this new Marxist approach laid down by Lektorsky and Schviriev (1971) consists of the following rules: (*1*) the element should be described from the point of view of its place in the wider context; (*2*) stress should be laid on functional attributes so that one and the same object should be described differently depending on the functions it fulfills in the wider system; (3) the functional prerequisites of the existence, continuity, and change of the system should be defined; (4) the mutual determination of the state of the whole by the attributes of elements, and of the attributes of elements by the states of the whole, should be examined; (5) for the majority of systems the assumptions of directive and purposeful organization should be accepted and the mechanical model dismissed as inadequate; and (6) the changes in the structural and functional properties of the system should be regarded as endogenous, and their source sought within the system's boundaries.

There seems to be no doubt that the systems approach may be truly considered as the constitutive methodological component of Marxist sociology. The application of systemic–functional models in the study of society constitutes the fundamental affinity between the Marxist and the functionalist orientations.

Chapter 16

CONCLUSION

Robert Merton once observed that the distinguishing mark of science as opposed to the arts is that the former should always disclose not only the ultimate result, but also the scaffolding. As the scaffolding of my argument might have gotten lost in the course of the discussion, I want now to review its fundamental points. For the reader who was patient and diligent enough to arrive at this page the legitimate way, by starting at the beginning, it will serve as a useful summary. And for the reader who starts reading books at the end, it will give some idea of whether reading it through is worth the time and effort.

First, I firmly believe that *sociology is, or at least should be, an empirical science*. It should be judged by the same criteria as any other empirical science, and it should set itself the same goals as any other empirical science (whether social or natural). The primary goal of empirical science is to provide empirically grounded *explanations* of phenomena and processes. Other goals of science, such as the prediction of phenomena and processes, as well as practical control over the course of events, are secondary in the sense that they may be fully achieved only when there exist adequate explanations. The notorious inefficiency of sociology in dealing with predictive and practical matters is due mainly, though not exclusively, to the scarcity of empirically grounded explanations. The construction of such explanations must be considered as the basic imperative of further development of our discipline·

Second, to construct an explanation is to answer the question "why?" concerning some determinate phenomena or processes. In order to be adequate the answer must satisfy certain criteria; it must be specified, logically valid, testable, empirically justified, pragmatically complete, semantically consistent, and unified. An *explanatory answer which satisfies all the criteria of adequacy is called a theory*. In effect, a theory is defined as a system of interconnected explanations. The theory of society is an explanatory system which provides an adequate answer to two basic questions: "Why do societies hold together and persist?" (Hobbesian problem of order and stability) and "Why do societies fall apart and change?" (Marxian problem of conflict and transformation).

Third, the prerequisite for the construction of a theory is the specification of a *conceptual model* of the domain of reality that is to be explained. A conceptual model is a set of assumptions defining the fundamental features of that domain. The *general assumptions* of the model constitute a frame of reference within which the determinate range of empirical variability is possible. The *particular assumptions* of the model signify concrete decisions as to the values of the variables, among those possible on all dimensions of variability permitted by the general assumptions. The first necessary step toward a theory of society consists of the specification of a conceptual model of society.

Fourth, the well-detailed, precise, and promising conceptual model for the construction of a theory of society is to be found in the tradition of the *functional orientation* in sociology and social anthropology. In order to be a viable instrument for theory construction, the systemic–functional model must be *generalized* and put in *relative* terms. It must not be considered as a set of definite, absolute assertions, but rather as a frame of reference delimiting a certain space, within which contingent empirical propositions may be formulated.

Fifth, there are 13 general assumptions which make up the general frame of reference of the systemic–functional model. These assumptions may be classified into five clusters giving rise to *five types of systemic–functional models*. Within each of the models some dimensions of possible empirical variability are generated, and consequently, several particular assumptions defining the alternative extreme values along each of the dimensions may be distinguished. (This is represented in Table 16.1.)

Sixth, the generalized systemic–functional models are *free from the*

TABLE 16.1

Systemic–Functional Models

Conceptual model	Frame of reference (general assumptions)	Dimensions of variability (particular assumptions)
I. Simple system	1. Plurality 2. Wholeness 3. Integration 4. Boundary	a. Reciprocity or exploitation b. Consensus or conflict c. Dependence or autonomy d. Isolation or context
II. Teleological system	5. Directive organization 6. Self-regulation	e. Universal or specific functionality f. Uniform or diverse functionality g. Equipotent or differential functionality h. Functional indispensability or structural alternatives i. Equilibrium or disequilibrium
III. Functional system	7. Double-level directive organization 8. Double-level self-regulation	j. Monofunctionality or multifunctionality k. Commensurate or contradictory requirements l. Constant or changing requirements
IV. Purposeful system	9. Rational purposefulness of elements 10. Integration of systemic goals and individual purposes	m. Sociocentric or egocentric images of man n. Intended or unintended functions o. Manifest or latent functions
V. Multiple system	11. Plurality of subsystems 12. Heterogeneity of subsystems 13. Boundary interchange	p. Unity or disunity of subsystems r. Integration or disintegration of subsystems

static and ahistoric biases usually found in older versions of functionalism. They are equally able to handle both the static and dynamic, historic and ahistoric, features of social reality. As a consequence, they may be equally useful in the solution of the basic problems of social theory: the problem of order and persistence, as well as the problem of conflict and change.

Seventh, the generalized systemic–functional models, though elaborated most explicitly within the functionalist orientation, are *implicitly present in the Marxian notion of society*, and particularly in his theory of socioeconomic formation. This aspect of Marxist thought is currently widely recognized and creatively developed by Marxist sociologists in Eastern Europe.

Finally, I believe that the so-called crisis of contemporary sociology is nothing but a new myth of the discipline, and that in fact there exists a solid foundation on which to base further, much needed theoretical efforts.

BIBLIOGRAPHY

Abel, T.
1952   The present status of social theory. *American Sociological Review*, **17**(2): 156–164.

Aberle, D. F., A. K. Cohen, A. Davis, M. Levy, and F. X. Sutton
1950   The functional prerequisites of society. *Ethics* **60**(1): 100–111.

Ackerman, C. and T. Parsons
1966   The concept of social system as a theoretical device. In *Concepts, Theory and Explanation in the Behavioral Sciences*, pp. 24–42, edited by G. J. DiRenzo. New York: Random House.

Ackoff, R. L.
1959   Games, decisions and organization. *General Systems* **4**: 145–150.

Addis, L.
1969   Freedom and the Marxist philosophy of history. In *Readings in the Philosophy of the Social Sciences*, edited by M. Brodbeck. New York: Macmillan.

Afanasyev, V. G.
1963   O printsipach klasifikacji cielostnych sistiem. [On the principles of classification of systemic wholes.] *Voprosy Filosofii* **5**: 21–43.

Afanasyev, V. G.
1968   *Nautschnoye upravlienye obschtschestvom.* [Scientific Management of Society.] Moscow: International Publishers.

Agassi, J.
1960   Methodological individualism. *British Journal of Sociology* **11**: 244–270.

Ajdukiewicz, K.
1965   *Logika pragmatyczna.* [Pragmatic Logic.] Warsaw: Polish Scientific Publishers.

Almond, G. A. and J. S. Coleman (eds.)
1960   *The Politics of the Developing Areas.* Princeton, New Jersey: Princeton Univ. Press.

Anderson, A. R. and O. K. Moore
  1966   Models and explanations in the behavioral sciences. In *Concepts, Theory and Explanation in the Behavioral Sciences*, pp. 79–92, edited by G. J. DiRenzo. New York: Random House.
Apostle, C. N.
  1967   Parsonian sociology. *Sociology and Social Research* 51(3): 275–286.
Apter, D. E.
  1968   *Some Conceptual Approaches to the Study of Modernization.* Englewood Cliffs, New Jersey: Prentice–Hall.
Aron, R.
  1968   *Main Currents in Sociological Thought,* I. New York: Doubleday.
Artanovsky, S. N.
  1964   K kritikie konciepcii funkcjonalizma i akkulturacii. [Toward the Critique of Functionalism and Acculturation.] *Voprosy Filosofii* 1: 115–123.
Bachitov, M. S.
  1963   Probliema pritschinnosci w socjologii i kritika funkcjonalizma. [The Problem of Causality in Sociology and the Critique of Functionalism.] *Voprosy Filosofii* 9: 78–88.
Bales, R. F.
  1951   *Interaction Process Analysis.* Reading, Massachusetts: Addison-Wesley.
Barber, B.
  1956   Structural–functional analysis: Some problems and misunderstandings. *American Sociological Review* 21: 129–135.
Beattie, J. H. M.
  1959   Understanding and explanation in social anthropology. *The British Journal of Sciology* 10(1): 45–60.
Beattie, J. H. M.
  1964   *Other Cultures: Aims, Methods and Achievements in Social Anthropology.* New York: Free Press.
Bennett, J. W. and M. M. Tumin
  1964   Some cultural imperatives. In *Cultural and Social Anthropology,* pp. 9–21, edited by P. B. Hammond. New York: Macmillan.
Berelson, B. and G. A. Steiner
  1964   *Human Behavior: An Inventory of Scientific Findings.* New York: Harcourt.
Berghe, van den, P.
  1963   Dialectic and functionalism; toward a theoretical synthesis. *American Sociological Review* 28(5).
Bergmann, G.
  1962   Purpose, function and scientific explanation. *Acta Sociologica* 5: 225–238.
Berrien, F. K.
  1968   *General and Social Systems.* New Brunswick, New Jersey: Rutgers Univ. Press.
Bertalanffy, von L.
  1968   *General System Theory.* New York: George Braziller.
Beshers, J. M.
  1957   Models and theory construction. *American Sociological Review* 22(1): 32–38.

Bialyszewski, H.
1968   Koncepcja systemu spolecznego w socjologii. [The Concept of a Social System in Sociology.] *Studia Socjologiczne*, 3/4: 179–216.
Bierstedt, R. ed.
1969   *A Design for Sociology: Scope, Objectives and Methods.* Philadelphia: American Academy of Political and Social Science, Monograph 9.
Biriukov, B.
1967   Objasnienije. [Explanation.] In *Filosofskaja Enciklopiedija*, Vol. IV, pp. 125–126, edited by F. W. Konstantinov.
Blain, R. R.
1970   A critique of Parsons' four function paradigm. *The Sociological Quarterly* 11(2): 157–168.
Blalock, H. M. and A. B. Blalock
1959   Toward a clarification of system analysis in the social sciences. *Philosophy of Science* 26(2): 84–92.
Blau, P.
1969   Sociological analysis; current trends and personal practice. *Sociological Inquiry* 39(2): 119–130.
Blau, P.
1969a   Objectives of sociology. In *A Design for Sociology*, pp. 43–71, edited by R. Bierstedt. Philadelphia: American Academy of Political and Social Science.
Blauberg, I. W. and G. E. Yudin (eds.)
1970   *Mietodologitsceskije Problemy Sistemnogo Issliedovanija.* [The Methodological Problems of System-Research.] Moscow: Izdatielstvo Nauka.
Bock, K.
1948   Discussion. *American Sociological Review* 2: 165.
Borgatta, E. F.
1960   Functionalism and sociology. *American Sociological Review* 25(2): 267–268.
Boskoff, A.
1957   Social change; major problems in the emergence of theoretical and research foci. In *Modern Sociological Theory in Continuity and Change*, pp. 260–302, edited by H. Becker and A. Boskoff, New York: Dryden Press.
Boskoff, A.
1964   Functional analysis as a source of a theoretical repertory and research tasks in the study of social change. In *Explorations in Social Change*, pp. 213–243, edited by G. K. Zollschan and W. Hirsch. Boston: Houghton Mifflin.
Boskoff, A.
1969   *Theory in American Sociology.* New York: Crowell.
Boulding, K.
1956   General systems theory: The skeleton of science. *General Systems* 1: 11–17.
Braithwaite, R. B.
1960   *Scientific Explanation.* London and New York: Cambridge Univ. Press.
Braithwaite, R. B.

1962   Models in the empirical sciences. In *Logic, Methodology and Philosophy of Science*, pp. 224–231, edited by E. Nagel, P. Suppes, and A. Tarski. Stanford: Stanford Univ. Press.

Bredemeier, H. C.
1955   The methodology of functionalism. *American Sociological Review* 20: 173–180.

Bredemeier, H. C. and R. M. Stephenson
1962   *The Analysis of Social Systems*. New York: Holt.

Breed, W.
1955   Social control in the newsroom: A functional analysis. *Social Forces* 33: 226–335.

Brodbeck, M.
1958   Methodological individualism: definition and reduction. *Philosophy of Science* 25: 1–22.

Brodbeck, M.
1959   Models, meaning and theories. In *Symposium on Sociological Theory*, pp. 373–403, edited by L. Gross. New York: Harper & Row.

Brodbeck, M.
1962   Explanation, prediction and imperfect knowledge. In *Minnesota Studies in the Philosophy of Science*, Vol. III, pp. 231–272, edited by H. Feigl and G. Maxwell. Minneapolis: Univ. of Minnesota Press.

Brodbeck, M.
1969   *Readings in the Philosophy of the Social Sciences*. New York: Macmillan.

Brown, R.
1963   *Explanation in Social Science*. London: Routledge–Kegan

Buckley, W.
1957   Structural–functional analysis in modern sociology. In *Modern Sociological Theory in Continuity and Change*, pp. 239–259, edited by H. Becker and A. Boskoff. New York: Dryden Press.

Buckley, W.
1958   Social stratification and the functional theory of social differentiation. *American Sociological Review* 23(4): 369–374.

Buckley, W.
1963   On equitable inequality. *American Sociological Review* 28(5): 799–801.

Buckley, W.
1967   *Sociology and Modern Systems Theory*. Englewood Cliffs, New Jersey: Prentice–Hall.

Buckley, W. (ed.)
1968   *Modern Systems Research for the Behavioral Scientist*. Chicago: Aldine.

Bunge, M.
1967   *Scientific Research*, Vols. I and II, Berlin: Springer Verlag.

Cancian, F.
1960   Functional analysis of change. *American Sociological Review* 25(6): 818–827.

Canfield, J.
1964   Teleological explanation in biology. *The British Journal for the Philosophy of Science* 14: 285–295.

Charvat, F.
1970   On the philosophical aspects of system concept in current sociological cognition. Prague (mimeographed).

Cohen, P. S.
1966   On models. *The British Journal of Sociology* 17: 70–77.

Cohen, P. S.
1968   *Modern Social Theory*. London: Routledge–Kegan.

Coser, L. A.
1956   *The Functions of Social Conflict*. New York: Free Press.

Coser, L. A.
1957   Social conflict and the theory of social change. *The British Journal of Sociology* 8: 197–207.

Coser, L. A.
1967   *Continuities in the Study of Social Conflict*. New York: Free Press.

Coser, L. A. and B. Rosenberg (eds.)
1964   *Sociological Theory*. New York: Macmillan.

Dahrendorf, R.
1968   *Essays in the Theory of Society*. Stanford: Stanford Univ. Press.

Davis, K.
1949   *Human Society*. New York: Macmillan.

Davis, K.
1959   The myth of functional analysis as a special method of sociology and anthropology. *American Sociological Review* 24: 757–773.

Davis, K. and W. E. Moore
1945   Some principles of stratification. *American Sociological Review* 10(2): 242–249.

Demerath, N. J.
1966   Synecdoche and structural-functionalism. *Social Forces* 44: 390–401.

Demerath, N. J. and R. A. Peterson
1967   *System, Change and Conflict*. New York: Macmillan.

Deutsch, K.
1951   Mechanism, teleology and mind. *Philosophy and Phenomenological Research* 12(2): 185–223.

Deutsch, K.
1966   *The Nerves of Government: Models of Political Communication and Control*. New York: Free Press.

DiRenzo, G. J. (ed.)
1966   *Concepts, Theory and Explanation in the Behavioral Sciences*. New York: Random House.

Dore, R. P.
1961   Function and cause. *American Sociological Review* 26: 843–853.

Ducasse, C. J.
1949   Explanation, mechanism and teleology. In *Readings in Philosophical Analysis*, pp. 540–544, edited by H. Feigl and W. Sellars. New York: Appleton.

Easton, D.
1953   *The Political System*. New York: Knopf.

Easton, D.
  1957   An approach to the analysis of political systems. *World Politics* **9**: 383–400.
Easton, D.
  1965a   *A Framework for Political Analysis.* Englewood Cliffs, New Jersey: Prentice–Hall.
Easton, D.
  1965b   *A Systems Analysis of Political Life.* New York: Wiley.
Eisenstadt, S. N.
  1971   Societal goals, systemic needs, social interaction and individual behavior; Some tentative explorations. In *Institutions and Social Exchange,* pp. 36–55, edited by H. Turk and R. L. Simpson. Indianapolis: Bobbs–Merrill.
Emmet, D.
  1958   *Function, Purpose and Powers.* London: Routledge–Kegan.
Evans–Pritchard, E. E.
  1954   *Social Anthropology.* London: Routledge–Kegan.
Fallding, H.
  1963   Functional analysis in sociology. *American Sociological Review* **28**(1): 5–13.
Fallding, H.
  1968   *The Sociological Task.* Englewood Cliffs, New Jersey: Prentice–Hall.
Faris, R. E. L. (ed.)
  1964   *Handbook of Modern Sociology.* Chicago: Aldine.
Feigl, H.
  1949   Some remarks on the meaning of scientific explanation. In *Readings in Philosophical Analysis,* pp. 510–514, edited by H. Feigl and W. Sellars. New York: Appleton.
Feigl, H. and M. Brodbeck
  1953   *Readings in the Philosophy of Science.* New York: Appleton.
Feigl, H. and G. Maxwell
  1962   *Minnesota Studies in the Philosophy of Science,* Vol. III. Minneapolis: Univ. of Minnesota Press.
Feigl, H. and W. Sellars (eds.)
  1949   *Readings in Philosophical Analysis.* New York: Appleton.
Feuer, L. S.
  1954   Causality in the social sciences. *Journal of Philosophy* **51**: 191–208.
Firth, R.
  1956   Function. In *Current Anthropology,* edited by W. L. Thomas. Chicago: Univ. of Chicago Press.
Firth, R.
  1957   *Man and Culture,* London: Routledge–Kegan.
Fletcher, R.
  1956   Functionalism as a social theory. *The Sociological Review* **4**:(1): 31–46.
Geertz, C.
  1957   Ritual and social change. *American Anthropologist* **59**: 32–54.
Gellner, E.
  1969   Explanations in history. In *Readings in the Philosophy of the Social Sciences,* edited by M. Brodbeck. New York: Macmillan.

Gershikov, V. I.
1970 On system character of the objects of social management. Novosibirsk (mimeographed).

Gibson, Q.
1960 *The Logic of Social Enquiry.* London: Routledge–Kegan.

Goldstein, L. J.
1957 The logic of explanation in Malinowskian anthropology. *Philosophy of Science* 24(2): 156–166.

Goode, W. I.
1951 *Religion among the primitives.* Glencoe, Illinois: Free Press.

Gouldner, A. W.
1959 Reciprocity and autonomy in functional theory. In *Symposium on Sociological Theory*, pp. 241–270, edited by L. Gross. New York: Harper & Row.

Gouldner, A. W.
1960 The norm of reciprocity; A preliminary statement. *American Sociological Review* 25(2): 161–178.

Gouldner, A. W.
1970 *The Coming Crisis of Western Sociology.* New York: Basic Books.

Griaznov, B. S., B. Dynin, and E. P. Nikitin
1967 Gnozieologiczieskije probliemy modielirowanija. [Gnoseological Problems of Model-Construction.] *Voprosy Filosofii* 2: 66–77.

Gross, L. (ed.)
1959 *Symposium on Sociological Theory.* New York: Harper & Row.

Gross, L. (ed.)
1967 *Sociological Theory: Inquiries and Paradigms.* New York: Harper & Row.

Hage, J.
1972 *Techniques and Problems of Theory-Construction in Sociology.* New York: Wiley.

Hagen, E. E.
1961 Analytical models in the study of social systems. *American Journal of Sociology* 67(2): 144–151.

Hall, A. D. and R. E. Fagen
1956 Definition of system. *General Systems* 1: 18–28.

Hammond, P. B. (ed.)
1964 *Cultural and Social Anthropology.* New York: Macmillan.

Harre, R.
1968 *An Introduction to the Logic of the Sciences,* New York: Macmillan

Harre, R.
1970 *The Principles of Scientific Thinking.* New York: Macmillan

Harsanyi, J. C.
1968 Individualistic and functionalistic explanations in the light of game theory. In *Problems in the Philosophy of Science*, edited by I. Lakatos and A. Musgrave. Amsterdam: Mart. Nijhoff.

Hempel, C. G.
1942 The function of the general laws in history. *Journal of Philosophy* 39: 35–48.

Hempel, C. G.
1959 The logic of functional analysis. In *Symposium on Sociological Theory,* pp. 270–310, edited by L. Gross. New York: Harper & Row.
Hempel, C. G.
1962 Deductive–nomological versus statistical explanation. In *Minnesota Studies in the Philosophy of Science,* edited by H. Feigl and G. Maxwell. Vol. III, pp. 98–169, Minneapolis: Univ. of Minnesota Press.
Hempel, C. G.
1965 *Aspects of Scientific Explanation.* New York: Free Press.
Hempel, C. G.
1966 *Philosophy of Natural Science.* Englewood Cliffs, New Jersey: Prentice–Hall.
Hempel, C. G. and M. Oppenheim
1953 Studies in the logic of explanation. In *Readings in the Philosophy of Science,* pp. 319–352, edited by H. Feigl and M. Brodbeck. New York: Appleton.
Hernes, G.
1971 *The Logic of Functional Analysis.* Bergen: Univ. of Bergen (mimeographed).
Hield, W.
1954 The study of change in social science. *British Journal of Sociology* **5:** 1–10.
Hoebel, E. A.
1954 *The Law of Primitive Man.* Cambridge, Massachusetts: Harvard Univ. Press.

Holt, R. T.
1965 A proposed structural–functional framework for political science. In *Functionalism in Social Sciences,* pp. 84–110, edited by D. Martindale. Philadelphia: American Academy of Political and Social Science.

Homans, G. C.
1950 *The Human Group.* New York: Harcourt.
Homans, G. C.
1961 *Social Behavior: Its Elementary Forms.* New York: Harcourt.
Homans, G. C.
1962 *Sentiments and Activities: Essays in Social Science.* New York: Free Press.
Homans, G. C.
1964 Contemporary theory in sociology. In *Handbook of Modern Sociology,* edited by R. E. L. Faris. Chicago: Aldine.
Homans, G. C.
1967 *The Nature of Social Science.* New York: Harcourt.
Homans, G. C.
1971 Bringing men back in. In *Institutions and Social Exchange,* edited by H. and R. L. Simpson. Indianapolis, Indiana: Bobbs Merrill.
Horovitz, I. L.
1962 Consensus, conflict and cooperation: A sociological inventory. *Social Forces* **41:** 177–188.

Hovard, R. B.
1971   Theoretical reduction: The limits and alternatives to reductive methods in scientific explanation. *Philosophy of the Social Sciences* 1: 83–100.
Huaco, G. A.
1963   A logical analysis of the Davis–Moore theory of stratification. *American Sociological Review* 28(5): 801–804.
Huaco, G. A.
1966   The functionalist theory of stratification. *Inquiry* 9(3): 215–240.
Isajiw, W. W.
1968   *Causation and Functionalism in Sociology.* New York: Shocken.
Israel, J.
1971   The principle of methodological individualism and Marxian epistemology. *Acta Sociologica* 14(3): 145–150.
Jahoda, M., M. Deutsch, and S. W. Cook
1951   *Research Methods in Social Relations,* Vol. I. New York: Dryden Press.
Janne, H.
1954   Fonction et finalite en sociologie. *Cahier Internationaux de Sociologie* 16: 50–67.
Kaberry, P.
1957   Malinowski's contribution to field-work methods and the writing of ethnography. In *Man and Culture,* edited by R. Firth. London: Routledge–Kegan.
Kallen, H.
1934   Functionalism. In *Encyclopaedia of the Social Sciences,* Vol. VI, pp. 523–535, edited by E. R. A. Seligman. New York: Macmillan.
Kaplan, A.
1964   *The Conduct of Inquiry.* San Francisco: Chandler.
Kaplan, A.
1965   Noncausal explanation. In *Cause and Effect,* pp. 145–155, edited by D. Lerner. New York: Free Press.
Kaplan, D. and R. A. Manners
1972   *Culture Theory.* Englewoods Cliffs, New Jersey: Prentice–Hall.
Kaplan, M. A.
1968   Systems theory and political science. *Social Research* 35(1): 30–47.
Kemeny, G.
1959   *A Philosopher Looks at Science.* Princeton, New Jersey: Van Nostrand Reinhold.
Klausner, S. Z. (ed.)
1967   *The Study of Total Societies.* New York: Praeger.
Kluckhohn, C.
1944   Navaho witchcraft. *Papers of the Peabody Museum* 22(2).
Kluckhohn, C.
1957   *Mirror for Man.* New York: Whittlesey House.
Kluckhohn, C.
1962   The concept of culture. In *Culture and Behavior,* pp. 19–73, edited by C. Kluckhohn. New York: Free Press.

Kluckhohn, C.
  1963 Parts and wholes in cultural analysis. In *Parts and Wholes*, pp. 111–133, edited by D. Lerner. New York: Free Press.
Kochanski, Z.
  1966 *Problem celowosci we wspolczesnej biologii.* [Problem of purposefulness in biology.] Warsaw: Ossolineum Publ.
Konstantinov, F. W., G. V. Osipov, and V. S. Siemionov
  1964 *Marksistskaja i burzuaznaja socjologia siewodnia.* [Marxist and Bourgeois Sociology Today.] Moscow: Izdatiels-two Nauka.
Krech, D., R. S. Crutchfield, and E. L. Ballachey
  1962 *Individual in Society.* New York: McGraw-Hill.
Krupp, S. R.
  1965 Equilibrium theory in economics and in functional analysis as types of explanation. In *Functionalism in the Social Sciences*, pp. 65–83, edited by D. Martindale. Philadelphia: American Academy of Political and Social Science.
Kuhn, A.
  1960 *The Study of Society; A Multidisciplinary Approach.* London: Oxford Univ. Press.
Kuhn, T. S.
  1970 *The Structure of Scientific Revolutions.* Chicago: Univ. of Chicago Press.
Lachenmeyer, C. W.
  1971 *The Language of Sociology.* New York: Columbia Univ. Press.
Lange, O.
  1962 *Calosc i rozwoj w swietle cybernetyki.* [Whole and Development from the Cybernetic Point of View.] Warsaw: Polish Scientific Publishers.
Lazarsfeld, P. F.
  1970 Sociology. In *Main Trends of Research in the Social and Human Sciences*, Vol. I, pp. 61–165. The Hague: Mouton.
Leach, E. R.
  1951 The structural implications of the matrilateral cross-cousin marriage. *Journal of the Royal Anthropological Institute* 81: 23–55.
Lehman, H. S.
  1964 Teleological explanation in biology: A discussion. *The British Journal for the Philosophy of Science* 15: 327–328.
Lehman, H. S.
  1966 R. K. Merton's concepts of function and functionalism. *Inquiry* 9(3): 274–283.
Lektorsky, W. A. and W. S. Schviriev
  1971 Aktualnyje filosofskije i mietodologitscheskye problyemy sistyemnogo podchoda. [Actual Philosophical and Methodological Problems of System-Approach.] *Voprosy Filosofii* 1: 123–131.
Lenin, V. I.
  1949 *Polnyje sobranije soczinienij.* [Complete Works.] Moscow.
Lenin, V. I.
  1956 *Zeszyty filozoficzne.* [Philosophical Notebooks.] Warsaw: Ksiazka i Wiedza.

Lenin, V. I.
1968 *Selected Works.* Moscow: Foreign Language Press.
Lerner, D. (ed.)
1963 *Parts and Wholes.* New York: Free Press.
Lerner, D.
1965 *Cause and Effect.* New York: Free Press.
Levy, M., Jr.
1952 *The Structure of Society.* Princeton, New Jersey: Princeton Univ. Press.
Levy, M. Jr.
1966 *Modernization and the Structure of Societies.* Princeton, New Jersey: Princeton Univ. Press.
Lockwood, D.
1956 Some remarks on the social system. *The British Journal of Sociology* **7**: 134–146.
Lockwood, D.
1964 Social integration and system integration. In *Explorations in Social Change,* pp. 244–257, edited by G. K. Zollschan and W. Hirsch. New York: Houghton Mifflin.
Lopreato, J.
1971 The concept of equilibrium; Sociological tantalizer. In *Institutions and Social Exchange,* pp. 309–343, edited by H. Turk and R. L. Simpson. Indianapolis: Bobbs Merrill.
Loomis, C. P. and Z. K. Loomis
1961 *Modern Social Theories.* Princeton, New Jersey: Van Nostrand, Reinhold.
Mace, C. A.
1949 Mechanical and teleological causation. In *Readings in Philosophical Analysis,* pp. 534–539, edited by H. Feigl and W. Sellars. New York: Appleton.
MacEwen, W. P.
1963 *The Problem of Social Scientific Knowledge.* Totowa, New Jersey: Bedminster Press.
Machlup, F.
1958 Equilibrium and disequilibrium: Misplaced concreteness and disguised politics. *The Economic Journal* **68**: 1–24.
Malewski, A.
1961 Dwa modele socjologii. [Two Models of Sociology.] *Studia Socjologiczne* **3**: 42–54.
Malewski, A.
1962 Z zagadnien ogolnej teorii zachowania. [The Problems of General Theory of Behavior.] *Studia Socjologiczne* **4**: 5–40.
Malewski, A.
1963 Szczeble ogolnosci teorii a proces wyjasniania. [Levels of Generalization and the Explanatory Process.] *Studia Socjologiczne* **2**: 63–84.
Malewski, A.
1964 *O zastosowaniach teorii zachowania.* [On the Applications of Theory of Behavior.] Warszawa: Polish Scientific Publishers.
Malinowski, B.
1922 *Argonauts of the Western Pacific:* New York: Dutton.

Malinowski B,
   1926   *Crime and Customs in Savage Society.* New York: Dutton.
Malinowski, B.
   1934   Culture. In *Encyclopaedia of the Social Sciences,* Vol. 4, edited by
          E. R. A. Seligman. New York: Macmillan.
Malinowski, B.
   1935   *Coral Gardens and Their Magic,* 2 vols. London: Allen & Unwin.
Malinowski, B.
   1936   Anthropology. In *Encyclopaedia Britannica,* 1st supplementary volume,
          pp. 131–140.
Malinowski, B.
   1954   *Magic, Science and Religion.* Garden City, New York: Doubleday.
Malinowski, B.
   1964   Anthropology. In *Sociological Theory,* edited by L. A. Coser and B.
          Rosenberg. New York: Macmillan.
Malinowski, B.
   1969   *A Scientific Theory of Culture and Other Essays.* London and New
          York: Oxford Univ. Press.
Manners, R. A. and D. Kaplan (eds.)
   1968   *Theory in Anthropology.* Chicago: Aldine.
Markarian, E. S.
   1969   Mietod analiza socjalnoj sistiemy. [The Method of Social System Analy-
          sis.] In *Socjologia i idieologia,* pp. 38–43, edited by E. A. Arab-Ogly.
          Moscow: Izdatielstwo Nauka.
Martindale, D.
   1960   *The Nature and Types of Sociological Theory.* Boston: Houghton Mifflin.
Martindale, D.
   1964   The roles of humanism and scientism in the evolution of sociology.
          In *Explorations in Social Change,* edited by G. K. Zollschan and W.
          Hirsch. Boston: Houghton Mifflin.
Martindale, D. (ed.)
   1965   *Functionalism in the Social Sciences.* Philadelphia: American Academy
          of Political and Social Sciences.
Martindale, D.
   1971   Talcott Parsons' theoretical metamorphosis from social behaviorism to
          macrofunctionalism. In *Institutions and Social Exchange,* pp. 165–174,
          edited by H. Turk and R. L. Simpson. Indianapolis: Bobbs–Merrill.
Marx, K.
   1956   *Selected Writings in Sociology and Social Philosophy,* edited by T. B.
          Bottomore. New York: McGraw-Hill.
Marx, K.
   1961   *Dziela wybrane.* [Selected Works.] Warszawa: Ksiazka i Wiedza.
Marx, K. and F. Engels
   1968   *Selected Works.* Moscow: Foreign Language Press.
McKinney, J. C.
   1957   Polar variables of type construction. *Social Forces* 35(4): 300–306.
Meadows, P.
   1957   Models, systems and science. *American Sociological Review* 22(1): 3–9.

Meehan, E. J.
1968   *Explanation in Social Science: A System Paradigm.* Homewood: Dorsey Press.
Merton, R. K.
1949   *Social Theory and Social Structure.* Glencoe, Illinois: Free Press.
Merton, R. K.
1967   *On Theoretical Sociology.* New York: Free Press.
Mills, C. W.
1959   Sociological Imagination. New York and London: Oxford Univ. Press.
Moore, B.
1967   The new scholasticism and the study of politics. In *System, Change and Conflict,* pp. 333–338, edited by N. J. Demerath and R. J. Peterson. New York: Free Press.
Mulkay, M. J.
1971   *Functionalism, Exchange and Theoretical Strategy.* London: Routledge–Kegan.
Mullins, N. C.
1971   *The Art of Theory: Construction and Use.* New York: Harper & Row.
Myrdal, G.
1953   The relation between social theory and social policy. *The British Journal of Sociology* 4(3): 210–242.
Nadel, S. F.
1957   Malinowski on magic and religion. In *Man and Culture,* pp. 189–208, edited by R. Firth. London: Routledge–Kegan.
Nagel, E.
1956   The formalization of functionalism. In *Logic Without Metaphysics,* pp. 247–283. Glencoe, Illinois: Free Press.
Nagel, E.
1961   *The Structure of Science.* New York: Harcourt, Brace & World.
Nagel, E.
1963   Wholes, sums and organic unities. In *Parts and Wholes,* pp. 135–155, edited by D. Lerner. New York: Free Press.
Nagel, E.
1965   Types of causal explanation in science In *Cause and Effect,* pp. 11–32, edited by D. Lerner. New York: Free Press.
Nagel, E., P. Suppes, and A. Tarski (eds.)
1962   *Logic, Methodology and Philosophy of Science.* Stanford: Stanford University Press.
Nikitin, E. P.
1963   Tipy naucznogo objasnienija. [Types of Scientific Explanation.] *Voprosy Filosofii* 10: pp. 30–39.
Nikitin, E. P.
1964   Struktura naucznogo objasnienija. [The Structure of Scientific Explanation.] In *Mietodologiczeskye problyemy sovryemyennoy nauki.* [Methodological problems of contemporary science.] Moscow: Izdatielstwo Nauka.
Nikitin, E. P.
1970   *Objasnienije: funkcya nauki.* [Explanation: the function of science.] Moscow: Izdatielstwo Nauka.

Nowak, S.
1965 *Studia z metodologii nauk spolecznych.* [Studies in the methodology of the social sciences.] Warsaw: Polish Scientific Publishers.

Nowak, S.
1970 *Metodologia badan socjologicznych.* [Methods of Sociological Research.] Warsaw: Polish Scientific Publishers.

Olickiy, A. A.
1968 Funkcjonalnye objasnyenye, pp. 130–134. [Functional Explanation.] Leningrad: Voprosy Filosofii i Psichologii.

Olszewska-Dyoniziak, B.
1964 Funkcjonalny model kultury w swietle niektorych osiagniec wspolczesnej antropologii i socjologii. [Functional model of culture from the point of view of modern anthropology and sociology.] *Etnografia Polska* 10: 31–60.

Ossowski, S.
1962 *O osobliwosciach nauk spolecznych.* [On the Peculiarities of Social Sciences.] Warsaw: Polish Scientific Publishers.

Parsons, T.
1948 The position of sociological theory. *American Sociological Review* 13(2): 156–164.

Parsons, T.
1951 *The Social System.* New York: Free Press.

Parsons, J.
1954 The Role of Theory in Social Research. *American Sociological Review* 19(2): 3–10.

Parsons, T.
1957 Malinowski and the theory of social systems. In *Man and Culture,* pp. 53–70, edited by R. Firth. London: Routledge–Kegan.

Parsons, T.
1964 *Essays in Sociological Theory.* New York: Free Press.

Parsons, T.
1965a An outline of the social system. In *Theories of Society,* pp. 30–79, edited by T. Parsons, E. Shils, K. E. Naegele, and J. R. Pitts. New York: Free Press.

Parsons, T.
1965b Cause and Effect in Sociology. In *Cause and Effect,* pp. 51–73, edited by D. Lerner. New York: Free Press.

Parsons, T.
1971a Levels of Organization and the Mediation of Social Interaction. In *Institutions and Social Exchange,* pp. 23–35, edited by H. Turk and R. L. Simpson. Indianapolis, Indiana: Bobbs–Merrill.

Parsons, T.
1971b Commentary. In *Institutions and Social Exchange,* pp. 380–400, edited by H. Turk and R. L. Simpson. Indianapolis, Indiana: Bobbs–Merrill.

Parsons, T. and E. A. Shils (eds.)
1951 *Toward a General Theory of Action.* New York: Harper & Row.

Parsons, T. and N. Smelser
1956 *Economy and Society.* New York: Free Press.

Piddington, R.
1957 Malinowski's theory of needs. In *Man and Culture*, pp. 33–51, edited by R. Firth. London: Routledge–Kegan.

Poggi, G.
1965 A main theme of contemporary sociological analysis; its achievements and limitations. *The British Journal of Sociology* 16(4): 283–294.

Popov, S. I.
1970 *Kritika sovryemyennoy burzuaznoj socjologii.* [The Critique of Contemporary Bourgeois Sociology.] Moscow.

Popper, K. R.
1960 *The Logic of Scientific Discovery.* London: Hutchinson.

Quine,W. V. and J. S. Ullian
1970 *The Web of Belief.* New York: Random House.

Radcliffe-Brown, A. R.
1922 *Andaman Islanders.* Cambridge: Cambridge Univ. Press.

Radcliffe-Brown, A. R.
1935 On the concept of function in social science. *American Anthropologist* 37: 3–21.

Radcliffe-Brown, A. R.
1952 *Structure and Function in Primitive Society.* New York: Free Press.

Radcliffe-Brown, A. R.
1958 *Method in Social Anthropology.* Chicago: Aldine.

Rapoport, A.
1967 Mathematical, evolutionary, and psychological approaches to the study of total societies. In *The Study of Total Societies*, pp. 114–143, edited by S. Z. Klausner. New York: Praeger.

Rex, J.
1961 *Key Problems of Sociological Theory.* London: Routledge & Kegan Paul.

Richards, A. J.
1957 The concept of culture in Malinowski's work. In *Man and Culture*, edited by R. Firth. London: Routledge–Kegan.

Robson, R. A. H.
1968 The present state of theory in sociology. In *Problems in the Philosophy of Science*, pp. 349–370, edited by J. Lakatos and A. Musgrave. Amsterdam: Martinus Nijhoff.

Rodner, K.,
1967 Logical foundations of social change theory. *Sociology and Social Research* 51(3): 287–301.

Rose, A. M.
1967 The relation of theory and method. In *Sociological Theory; Inquiries and Paradigms*, pp. 207–219, edited by L. Gross. New York: Harper & Row.

Rudner, R. S.
1966 *Philosophy of Social Science.* Englewood Cliffs, New Jersey: Prentice Hall.

Russell, E. S.
1945 *The Directiveness of Organic Activities.* Cambridge: Cambridge Univ. Press.

Sadovsky, V. N.
  1966 Metodologiczne problemy badan kompleksowych. [Methodological prob-
         lems of ·complex research.] In *Socjologia w ZSRR.* [Sociology in USSR.]
         Warszawa: Panstwowe Wydawnictwo Ekonomic: ne.
Sadovsky, V. N. and E. T. Yudin
  1967 O spiecifikie mietodologiczeskogo podchoda k issliedowaniju sistiem i
         struktur. [On the specificity of methodological approach to systems and
         structures.] In *Logika i mietodologia nauki.* [Logic and Methodology
         of Science.] Moscow: Izdatielstwo Nauka.
Scheffler, I.
  1958 Thoughts on teleology. *The British Journal for the Philosophy of Science*
         9(6): 265–284.
Scheffler, I.
  1963 *The Anatomy of Inquiry: Philosophical Studies in the Philosophy of
         Science.* New York: Knopff.
Schrag, C.
  1967 Elements of theoretical analysis in sociology. In *Sociological Theory:
         Inquiries and Paradigms,* pp. 220–253, edited by L. Gross. New York:
         Harper & Row.
Schrag, C.
  1967a Philosophical issues in the science of sociology. *Sociology and Social
         Research* 51(3): 361–372.
Schwartz, R. D.
  1955 Functional alternatives to inequality. *American Sociological Review*
         20: 424–430.
Scott, M. B.
  1966 Functional foibles and the analysis of social change. *Inquiry* 9(3):
         205–214.
Shanin, T.
  1972 Units of sociological analysis. *Sociology* 6(3): 352–367.
Simon, H. A.
  1970 *The Sciences of the Artificial.* Cambridge, Massachusetts: Harvard Univ.
         Press.
Simon, H. A. and A. Newell
  1956 Models; their uses and limitations. In *The State of the Social Sciences,*
         pp. 66–83, edited by L. D. White. Chicago: Aldine.
Simpson, R. L.
  1956 A modification of the functional theory of social stratification. *Social
         Forces* 35.
Sjoberg, G.
  1967 Contradictory functional requirements and social systems. In *System,
         Change, and Conflict,* pp. 339–345, edited by N. J. Demerath and
         R. A. Peterson. Glencoe, Illinois: Free Press. Originally published in
         the *Journal of Conflict Resolution* 4(2): 198–208, 1960.
Sjoberg, E. and L. D. Cain
  1971 Negative values, countersystem models, and the analysis of social sys-
         tems. In *Institutions and Social Exchange,* pp. 212–232, edited by H.
         Turk and R. L. Simpson. Indianapolis, Indiana: Bobbs–Merrill.

Smelser, N. J.
1968   *Studies in Sociological Explanation.* Englewood Cliffs, New Jersey: Prentice-Hall.
Smelser, N. J.
1969   The optimum scope of sociology. In *A Design For Sociology: Scope, Objectives and Methods,* pp. 1–21, edited by R. Bierstedt. Philadelphia: American Academy of Political and Social Science.
Smelser, N. J. and W. T. Smelser
1964   *Personality and Social Systems.* New York: Wiley.
Soares, G. A. D.
1968   Marxism as a general sociological orientation. *The British Journal of Sociology* 19(4): 356–374.
Sorokin, P.
1965   Sociology of yesterday, today and tomorrow. *American Sociological Review* 30(6): 833–843.
Sorokin, P.
1966   *Sociological Theories of Today.* New York: Harper & Row.
Sorokin, P.
1967   Causal-functional and logico-meaningful integration. In *System, Change and Conflict,* pp. 99–114, edited by N. P. Demerath and R. A. Peterson. New York: Free Press.
Spiro, M. E.
1961   Social systems, personality and functional analysis. In *Studying Personality Cross-Culturally,* pp. 93–127, edited by B. Kaplan. Evanston, Illinois: Row, Paterson.
Spiro, M. E.
1968   Causes, functions, and cross-cousin marriage: An essay in anthropological explanation. In *Theory in Anthropology,* pp. 105–115, edited by R. A. Manners and D. Kaplan. Chicago: Aldine.
Stinchcombe, A. L.
1963   Some empirical consequences of the Davis-Moore theory of stratification. *American Sociological Review* 28(5): 805–808.
Stinchcombe, A. L.
1968   *Constructing Social Theories.* New York: Harcourt.
Swanson, G. E.
1953   The approach to a general theory of action by Parsons and Shils. *American Sociological Review* 18: 125–134.
Swanson, J. W.
1967   On models. *The British Journal for the Philosophy of Science* 17(4): 297–312.
Sztompka, P.
1968   O pojeciu modelu w socjologii. [On the notion of model in sociology.] *Studia Socjologiczne* 1: 27–58.
Sztompka, P.
1969a   Dwa pojecia celowosci w socjologii. [Two concepts of purpose in sociology.] *Studia Socjologiczne* 3: 45–69.
Sztompka, P.
1969b   Statyczna i dynamiczna wersja funkcjonalizmu. [Static and dynamic version of functionalism.] *Studia Socjologiczne* 4: 157–191.

Sztompka, P.
1969c   Teleological language in sociology. *The Polish Sociological Bulletin*
         2: 56–69.
Sztompka, P.
1971a   The logic of functional analysis in sociology and social anthropology.
         Quality and Quantity: European Journal of Methodology 5(2): 369–388.
Sztompka, P.
1971b   Some conditions of applicability of sociological knowledge. *The Polish
         Sociological Bulletin* 1: 5–16.
Sztompka, P.
1971c   O pojeciu teorii w socjologii. [On the notion of theory in sociology.]
         Studia Socjologiczne 3: 19–51.
Sztompka, P.
1971d   *Metoda funkcjonalna w socjologii i antropologii spolecznej.* Warsaw:
         Ossolineum Publishers.
Sztompka, P.
1972   Strategia budowy teorii w socjologii. [Strategy of theory construction in
         sociology.] *Studia Socjologiczne* 1: 1–38.
Sztompka, P.
1973   Teoria: wyjasnienie. [Theory and Explanation.] Warsaw: Polish Scientific
         Publishers.
Taylor, K. W.
1970   A Paradigm for causal analysis. *The Sociological Quarterly* 11(2):
         169–180.
Topolski, J.
1968a   *Metodologia historii.* [Methods of History.] Warsaw: Polish Scientific
         Publishers.
Topolski, J.
1968b   Zalozenia metodologiczne "Kapitalu" Marksa. [Methodological assump-
         tions of Marx' *Das Kapital.*] *Studia Filozoficzne,* 4: 3–33.
Topolski, J. (ed.)
1970   *Zalozenia metodologiczne Kapitalu Marksa.* [Methodological Assumptions
         of Marx' *Das Kapital.*] Warsaw: Ksiazka i Wiedza.
Tumin, M. M.
1953   Some principles of stratification: A critical analysis. *American Sociological
         Review* 18: 387–394.
Turk, H. and R. L. Simpson (eds.)
1971   *Institutions and Social Exchange.* Indianapolis, Indiana: Bobbs–Merrill.
Wallace, W. L.
1969   *Sociological Theory.* Chicago: Aldine.
Warshay, L. H.
1971   The current state of sociological theory; diversity, polarity, empiricism
         and small theories. *The Sociological Quarterly* 1: 23–45.
Whitaker, I.
1965   The nature and value of functionalism in sociology. In *Functionalism
         in the Social Science,* pp. 127–143, edited by D. Martindale. Philadel-
         phia: American Academy of the Political and Social Science.

Willer, D. E.
   1967   *Scientific Sociology; Theory and Method.* Englewood Cliffs, New Jersey:
          Prentice–Hall.
Wrong, D.
   1961   The oversocialized conception of man in modern sociology. *American
          Sociological Review* **26**(2): 183–193.
Zetterberg, H. L.
   1954   *On Theory and Verification in Sociology.* Stockholm: Almquist.
Zetterberg, H. L.
   1962   *Social Theory and Social Practice.* Totowa, New Jersey: The Bedminster
          Press.
Zollschan, G. K. and W. Hirsch (eds.)
   1964   *Explorations in Social Change.* Boston: Houghton Mifflin.

AUTHOR INDEX

Numbers in italics refer to the pages on which the complete references are listed. Additional sources not cited in text can be found in the Bibliography.

SUBJECT INDEX